Widowed and Young... Learning a new WAY of life

Lisa Hennessy

PublishAmerica

Baltimore

First printing

ISBN: 1-59286-524-0
PUBLISHED BY PUBLISHAMERICA BOOK
PUBLISHERS
www.publishamerica.com
Baltimore

Printed in the United States of America

This book is dedicated to my husband, Pat, who has been supportive of this book and me and to my two precious children, Brandon and Danielle, who made my life worth living.

Thank You's: I want to thank all of my family and friends for their love, support and the medical community, especially the Alamo Orthopedic Society, Ellie Carey and

Widowed Persons Service of Tarrant County, for providing a place for the widowed and young.

Contents:

Author's Foreward

I am not a licensed counselor nor do I have a degree in Thanantology, but I do have life experience with death. I know what it is like to suddenly become a widow without a moment's notice. This book is based on both my own personal experiences and those of other kindred spirits who, as painful as it was, graciously opened their hearts to me and other widowed people in our Widowed and Young support group.

My hope for this book is that it will help validate some of the feelings of widowhood such as loneliness, despair, guilt, frustration, for example and support other widowed people in their healing process.

The title of this book stems from the support group that I started through Widowed Persons Service of Tarrant County called Widowed and Young or WAY. I chose the acronym WAY because God truly led the way for me with this endeavor. I knew from the day of John's death that God was going to use my tragedy to help others in similar circumstances.

Isaiah 42:16 I will lead the blind by ways they have not known, along unfamiliar paths I will guide them; I will turn darkness into light before them and make the rough places smooth.

Introduction

In October 1994, at the age of 29, John Gardemal signed a contract with a hospital in Henderson, Texas to go into private practice in orthopedic surgery. During our four-and-one half years of marriage, we had to live paycheck-to-paycheck on the meager salary provided to residents in training. What kept us going during these tough times was knowing that one day all of the long hours and hard work would eventually be rewarded when we went into private practice. When we signed that contract in October, all of our dreams were starting to come true. The struggle was over. Our financial hardships were lightened.

Anticipating our new life, we started to buy new things, including a home in East Texas. We were having it remodeled to be ready for move-in in mid-June, 1995. In March, we learned we were having our second child. In May, right after our son, Brandon's second birthday, I had a sonogram. It detected the life of a little girl. John had always wanted a little girl. We had even both agreed on a name for her, Danielle. This was quite a feat considering we couldn't agree on Brandon's name until three weeks before his birth.

Our marriage was at an all time high. We were so excited about our new job, new house, new baby and our new life.

Everything in my life seemed perfect to me. I felt like I had the fairy tale marriage. At this time, I could not have ever imagined a better life. I was so happy and so was John.

June 16, 1995, a day that will forever be etched in my mind. We were at a meeting/vacation in Cabo San Lucas, Mexico with three other couples from the orthopedic residency program in San Antonio, Texas, where John was completing his training. We had two more weeks before he was finished and off to Henderson, Texas to start our new life. This was to be our last big vacation before our move. The moving trucks were scheduled to move us from San Antonio to Henderson on June 19th.

We arrived in Mexico on Tuesday afternoon on June 13th. We were all having so much fun and enjoying our lives to the fullest. On Friday morning of June 16th, John had meetings to attend. He had the opportunity to play golf, but decided to go snorkeling with the other people in our group. It was a beautiful, sunny day. The perfect weather for snorkeling, or so we thought. Eleven of us took a boat out to Lover's Beach, which according to guest services at our hotel was "the best place to snorkel."

The boat ride to the beach was rough. We got out of the boat on the Sea of Cortez, but the waters on this part of the beach were much too rough for snorkeling. John and four other men from our group put down their snorkeling equipment and walked to the other side of the beach, which was the Pacific Ocean. While they did this, the rest of the group stayed with the snorkeling equipment. The guys wanted to see the famous "arch" they had seen in all of the literature about Cabo San Lucas. What they had not read is that the Pacific side of the beach was much more dangerous.

Within just a few minutes, a man came running to our group and said there was some trouble with some guys on the other side of the beach. I thought that maybe some men, not ours, were having a fight. The last thing I thought was that our men were the ones in trouble. One by one, the people left our group to check out what was happening on the other side of the beach. After a while, I was left standing alone watching our belongings. As I looked around at my solitude, I got this sick feeling in my stomach that something was wrong. I had a wave of panic that something had happened to John, so I started running to where the rest of our group was. My friend, Todd, was running toward me. That was when I knew something was wrong with John, because otherwise he would have been coming to check on me. Out of breath, Todd came to me and embraced me. Through tears he said, "I did everything I could, Lisa. I had a hold of his arm and told him, "get up and run John" and he looked up at me and said, "I can't, I can't." Then a wave took him away and I could not keep a hold of him. I am so sorry Lisa."

Apparently, they were walking in ankle-to-knee deep water behind some rocks with their backs to the water, when a huge wave swept the five men deep into the water. Three were able to make it to safety. John and one other man drowned. I was watching the belongings, so I did not actually see this happen. This is what I heard from the three that survived. Those who survived don't know how they did. They told me the waters were treacherous with a deadly undertow. Every time they could feel sand under their feet, they would get knocked down by another wave and taken back into the ocean.

This moment was like a big nightmare. I thought, "This can't be happening to me. This isn't really happening." As I stood on that beach, I watched my husband's body face down in the ocean going up and down in the swells of the ocean. He was like that for approximately thirty minutes, maybe longer before the rescue boats could get to his body. At this point, I prayed that God spare his life, but knew it was in vain, because of the amount of time he had been without oxygen. I always heard about those "miracle" stories where someone should have died but miraculously lived, why wouldn't this apply to John?

On the way back to the docks, we heard that the boats got both of the bodies and one of them still had a pulse. I knew it was John. He was going to make it! He **would** be one of those miracles! There was still hope! I was able to briefly hold John's hand when they first took him out of the boat. I asked John to not give up for our children. I told him he had to see our baby girl. He couldn't die! I watched in desperation our friends performing CPR on him. They had to stick this big plastic tube down his throat to try and get out all of the water that had filled his lungs. It was a horrific image to see my husband, who was so full of life and vitality one minute, lying blue and lifeless on the docks with his clothing ripped off of him. We all knew if they revived him he would be brain dead since he had been without oxygen for so long, but they still tried.

An ambulance came and took John to one of the two hospitals in Cabo San Lucas. One or two of the guys went in the ambulance to continue performing CPR. They were taking John to the hospital that had the most "modern" medical equipment. The other man was taken to the hospital that lacked the medical equipment since he was already pronounced dead. Somehow we were able to get to the hospital where they transported John. My friend, Elgene, and I had no idea where to go. In our limited, broken Spanish we tried to tell the cab driver where to go and he got us to the right hospital.

Mexico's version of a hospital wouldn't even be considered

a clinic here. Not to mention their "modern" medical equipment wouldn't be used anywhere here in the states because it was so old and dated. I sat in this dark, dingy Mexican hospital waiting in vinyl pea green chairs. After about ten minutes, my friends came out with their heads hung low and told me that John was gone and handed me his watch. Fortunately for me, he left his rings in the safe at the hotel, because the other man's wedding band was stolen somewhere between the boat ride and the hospital.

"John's gone?" This couldn't be true. What a blow! I kept thinking, "They can do it. They can save John." As I sat in those pea green chairs I thought, "I am going to walk into that room and John is going to be sitting up smiling saying, "Scared you, didn't I?" Of course none of that happened. John was dead. I was numb. I couldn't feel any grief or sadness because I was so much in shock. Again, I could not believe this was happening to me. It had to be a mistake.

Those next twelve hours are quite a blur to me. I had to make the calls to the states to tell the family what had happened. I stood outside the District Attorney's office at a pay phone. Some kind stranger from the orthopedic meeting had heard about what had happened and came to help us. He took out his calling card and dialed all the calls for me. I got the answering machine for the first three phone calls. I didn't leave any messages.

The fourth phone call was to my brother, Vince, who also lived in San Antonio, not far from John and I. His wife, Sonia, also my very best friend, answered the phone. I didn't want to call her because she was also pregnant and having a difficult pregnancy. I didn't want to burden her with having to make all of the phone calls. All I remember saying to her in a matter-of-fact voice was "John is dead." All I could hear from her was

"Oh, my God, Oh, my God, no, no, no, Lisa." I asked her to get hold of John's family and my family to let them know what was happening. I also think I told her I wanted my brother, Vince with me in Cabo San Lucas, because at this time, I had no idea how long I would be in this foreign country.

Because of the bureaucracy in Mexico, I had to go to the Mexican District Attorney's office for depositions. We had a translator from the hotel help us. Being in a foreign country was so frustrating. The depositions had to be typed with a manual typewriter with carbon copies. It seemed to take forever to get this done. I remember someone saying, "Does Lisa have to sit here and listen to all of this?" They said, "No." I was glad since it was agonizing for me to listen to all of the details of what had just transpired. This was still so surreal to me. I was only going through the motions at this time.

The American Counsel was also called in to help expedite the whole process. Once she showed up at the District Attorney's office, things began to run smoother. She had to take me back to the hospital to give the coroner the information needed for the death certificate. I also had to meet with the funeral director to arrange the embalming and the casket so we could get the body on the plane and home the next morning. I will never forget the American counsel telling the funeral director what had happened and his response to her was "another one?" Apparently, another American had drowned in that same spot the prior week. My friend who was with me understood their Spanish, so they were shocked when she responded, "Another one?"

Money apparently talks in Mexico, because we were able to get John's body out of the country within a twelve-hour period. The pharmaceutical company that sponsored the trip along with the hotel obviously had some connections and assured me that I would not be flying back to Texas without John's body. So, on the afternoon of June 16th, 1995, at the young age of twenty-eight, I became a widow.

These next several chapters describe a multitude of emotions. These emotions range from pain and sorrow to joy and celebration. So, why does death catch us by surprise? Everyone experiences it at some point in his or her life. Before vaccinations it was quite common for people to die from childhood illnesses. Death was not uncommon for younger people during these times. So, why is everyone so shocked and ill-prepared for an early death? Why? Because we think we are immune to it. We don't think that it will happen to us. We make believe that death doesn't exist so when it does come early, we are shocked. We don't expect it to happen to us, so we are not prepared when it does. However, there is hope and our lives eventually move forward.

I have learned that there is no right or wrong way to deal with grief. All of us choose our own path to follow. I am merely sharing how I dealt with my grief. My hope is that another young widowed person can pick up this book, relate to my thoughts and feelings and understand that they are not absolutely alone. They can survive the crisis, because I did. *Psalm 130:5 I wait for the Lord, my soul waits, and in his words I put my hope.*

Chapter One

Death Hits Me Full Force

Psalm 116:3 The cords of death entangled me, the anguish of the grave came upon me; I was overcome by trouble and sorrow.

Overwhelmed

At first, I was blinded by my own grief and could not see beyond it. All I could see was darkness. There was no longer the light at the end of the tunnel. Even though things seemed so dark in my life, I found a faith that I didn't know existed. I felt God directing me with all of the decisions that needed to be made.

The plane ride back to Texas was tortuous. I never imagined that I would be bringing my twenty-nine year old husband home from our vacation in a casket. He was supposed to be sitting next to me on the plane, not in a casket with all of the baggage. Because of the circumstances, the airline bumped me to first class. That was not the way I wanted to be sitting in first class. I would have much rather been in coach with a husband who was alive.

My in-laws were meeting me at the airport with my son, Brandon. I knew that they were expecting John to walk off the plane with me. Even though they were told what happened, I am sure they were clinging to the hope that someone had misinformed them. I knew the feeling. Walking off that plane without John was one of the hardest things I have ever had to do. All I wanted to do was to see my son and embrace him. I yearned to see his little smiling face. I had to be strong for him. As soon as I saw him, I had to plaster a smile on my face. Holding and hugging him was the only thing that gave me happiness. He was the only tangible thing that I had left of John. It was so hard to not break down and cry at this time, but I did not want to confuse him.

Since my brother Vince and his wife, Sonia, were in San Antonio, I had them go to our house and pick out my favorite sport coat, pants, shirt and tie of John's. I wanted him buried in something nice. Along with that, I asked them to bring some pictures for a collage. I hated to ask them to do these things, because they were hurting just as much as I was. We were like one big family all living in San Antonio together. Vince and John were like brothers.

I had so many decisions to make about the funeral and burial. I didn't know what to do. I went back and forth on whether or not I should bury John with his wedding ring and Texas A&M class ring. I finally decided to keep his class ring for Brandon, because if he goes to Texas A&M they can melt it down for his ring. I thought I would bury him with his wedding ring because it was a symbol of our love. Even though John's body would disintegrate, the ring never would. That gold wedding band is eternal, just like our love. I had to remind myself that the vows I took were "Until death do us part."

Because of my feelings for the wedding ring, I told the funeral director that I wanted to put the ring on John. He asked if I wanted to do it myself or have him do it. I told him that I would do it. Fortunately, he stood by my side as I struggled with shaking hands to place the ring on his cold limp hand. I broke down and could not do it. I handed him the ring and told him he would have to do it. I wanted so badly to place the ring on John's finger as I had on our wedding day, but it was much too difficult for me to do.

After viewing John's body, I decided to have a closed casket. In Mexico, the embalming process is different, so John did not look like John to me. They didn't even shave his face. His face was swollen. His hair was slicked back like Dracula, not to mention he would have never wanted anyone to see him with that much make-up. I knew that he would not want anyone to remember him that way. Since John and I had never talked about this, I had no idea whether I should bury him or cremate him. I just did what I thought he would have done for me.

I chose to let Brandon come with my family and me to the "viewing." The casket was closed, so I had to explain to him what was happening. I told him, "Daddy had died and gone to Heaven. His body was in this casket, but his soul had gone to Heaven to be with God." I then picked up Brandon, walked over to the casket and I had him put a picture of himself on the casket. The picture frame contained a recording of Brandon's voice saying, "I love you." This was placed inside the casket after the viewing.

I really thought that Brandon was oblivious to what was happening since he was only twenty-five months old, but I was wrong. At bedtime that evening I asked him if he knew where his Daddy was. He said, "Daddy's in Heaven…Daddy's in a casket." I didn't think he was listening to me earlier but, clearly, he was. He still didn't understand the ramifications of everything that had happened, but he did understand that his daddy was no longer here with us.

On that funeral day, both my heart and body were draped in black. I felt so hopeless. I very vaguely remember that day. I couldn't even tell you whom I had as pallbearers. I was so consumed with grief. I still could not believe that all of this was *really* happening to me. This was still a bad, bad dream. I was going to wake up soon and it would all be over, wouldn't it? When John and I were making the plans for our new life after residency training, I never thought or imagined these were contingency plans. These were our life plans. This was not supposed to happen until our "golden years." This doesn't happen to someone my age or John's age!

This was hard to accept because I had no choice in the matter. I never did wake up from that dream because it was reality. I did not want to accept that it could happen to me or to anyone I knew. It happens to other people! You read about it in the paper. You see it on television. This is not real. It can't be true! I am not a widow at the age of twenty-eight! I am not a single, pregnant mom! *I'm not, I'm not, I'm not!* I felt so cheated that John had died, not only for me, but especially the children. Death came much to early for him.

Shock was the best part of my grief. It was when I felt numb and felt nothing. It took me a few hours after John's death before I could really cry. I felt quite a bit of guilt because of this. Wasn't I supposed to cry when it first happened? What was wrong with me? As I look back now, I realize that shock was a gift that God gave me to cope with the death. As the shock dissipated, the hard part of the grieving began. I felt my life was hopeless. I knew that there was no pill that could ease this pain.

I was overwhelmed with all the decisions I had to make.

What to do with his body, what to do at the funeral service, writing thank-you notes, moving, Brandon, my life! I had so many problems to solve now. What seemed to be a rather easy life changed dramatically for me within seconds. Being a pregnant widow with a young child went way beyond just grief. I had so much more to deal with in addition to mourning John's death.

Feeling overwhelmed with my grief left me without the energy or knowledge to handle instrumental tasks such as my finances or housing situation. Since John and I had recently purchased the home in Henderson I had two choices. First, I could move to a new town where I knew very few people. The second choice was to move back to my hometown, Arlington and live with my mom and dad. Had John and I purchased the mortgage insurance for the home in Henderson, I might have chosen to live in the new home. But, again, this was not a contingency that John and I had entertained, so mortgage insurance seemed unnecessary at that time. I felt what was true of my life last week, was no longer true today.

I decided that the best thing for us was to sell the home in Henderson. My son and I moved back to Arlington to live with my mom and dad. My parents let me move some of my furniture into their home, so it would feel more like home to Brandon. We both needed some stability and familiarity in our lives. That was the best decision I made. I continued to make house payments, utility payments and maintenance on a home where I never resided. I had already notified the post office to forward my mail to Henderson. All of the remodeling was done for nothing. I never got to enjoy it.

I made some very hasty decisions that I know regret. Since I was in the process of moving, I did not want to have to go through all of John's personal belongings more than once. I gave a lot of things away that I later wished I would have kept. I didn't want to have to deal with any of it. I didn't care if someone wanted his power tools. I didn't care if someone took all of his camping and fishing gear. These were material things that weren't going to bring John back to me. However, looking back, there were some things I wished I had kept for the children. My advice to anyone going through something like this is to wait. Once you give it away, it is difficult to tell someone, even a good friend or family member, that you now want it for yourself.

I often thought and still think about John and what he must have been thinking when he was struggling for his life. The month before his death, Susan Smith drowned her two sons. I remember watching the news with John and him saying, "That has got to be the worst way for a person to die...drowning. You know you are going to die and there is nothing you can do about it." Knowing this really bothered me, because in his eyes drowning was the worst way for him to die. I wanted to believe that John was hurt and that he didn't suffer, but I know he was conscious when our friend, Todd, last saw him. After approximately forty-five minutes, he still had a pulse. This tells me that he hung on until the very last minute. He didn't want to give up on his life. I just pray that God was holding John's hand during this and he felt His presence and not pain.

Grief

Grieving is a healing process. It is not easy and it sure isn't pain free, but it is necessary. I learned, delaying grief only caused more suffering once I decided to confront my loss. I tried to run for as long as I could, but eventually I had to face it. I could only run for so long before my grief caught up with me.

When it did, it hit me like a brick wall. WHAM!

I hit my brick wall four months later when my daughter, Danielle, was born. I could no longer run from my grief and pretend I was on vacation "visiting" my parents. My daughter was born to a single mom and I had to accept that. This was my harsh reality when the admitting nurse asked "Are you married or single?" I broke down crying, "I am widowed." I remember my father, also there with me crying by my side. This emotional time in the hospital was difficult for both of us. This was now a truth that I had to accept. I was giving birth to my daughter without her father.

Reality was that John was not in the delivery room with me. Reality was that John would never be a part of Danielle's life. Reality was that I was now a single parent with no one to relieve me at the end of the day. Reality was there was no one to share the special moments with Brandon and Danielle. Reality was an empty spot at the dinner table. Reality was a lonely and empty bed at night. These were my realities and not realities that I wanted.

Because I could no longer run from these "realities," I knew it was time to seek some professional help. I could not stop crying after Danielle's birth. I knew something had to be wrong with me. I was so depressed. Five months after John's death, when Danielle was only a few weeks old, I finally sought one-on-one counseling. I was convinced that she would tell me I needed to be put on antidepressants and refer me to another doctor or tell me I needed some major therapy for this depression. To my surprise she told me that I was not going crazy. She said that I was a normal grieving person, whose husband had died and had just given birth to a baby. It felt so good to hear from a professional that I was "normal," because I sure didn't feel like it.

I was in a state of inertia. I was not living in the present or future. I was existing. "Time heals wounds." Really? What is time? When will time heal these deep wounds? Yes, time enabled me to deal with the death of my husband, but sometimes I wondered what time was. Time seemed motionless. I wasn't moving forward or backward.

Tears helped me to relieve the stress of my grief. By not crying, I was holding on to my pain. As hard as it was to cry and experience the pain, it had to be done. There were times when I literally thought that my heart-wrenching sobs were going to cause a miscarriage. I knew I had to be hurting my baby by these crying bouts. I had always heard "crying makes you feel better." If this was true, why did I feel so bad and lousy when I was done? I felt worse than before when I thought I was "doing so well."

There was not too much sleep in the early days of grief. There was too much going through my mind. As soon as I shut my eyes, all I could see was John's body floating up and down in the waves. I had a hard time getting beyond this horrible image. Eventually I was able to close my eyes and not see that; however, I still didn't sleep just because my eyes were shut.

Driving is a scary thing for a grieving person. Once I would get to where I was going, I would wonder how I actually arrived. I didn't remember driving past all of the places I would have normally noticed. If someone had pulled out in front of me, I wouldn't have seen him or her. I thank God for watching over me while I drove. A grieving person is dangerous on the road, oblivious to her surroundings. I looked forward to my car drives, because my car was my refuge. At first, my car was the only place I felt "safe" to cry. Living at home with my parents put the pressure on me to be strong in front of them.

Anger?

I wasn't ever angry with God for what happened, but I got mad at a lot of other people. For instance, it was very difficult to read so many of these grief books written by a professional who hadn't ever experienced this kind of loss, or going to a "general" grief recovery group for all types of losses. I know the man facilitating the grief recovery group I attended had good intentions, but I had a hard time accepting that he knew what I was feeling. He was married and was having a full life with his wife and children. How could he possibly know my pain when he had not ever experienced it? I thought I should be the one up in front of this group "teaching." I knew that one day, when I was ready, I would. Unfortunately, no one knows the grief until they themselves have experienced it.

I attempted this "general" grief recovery group shortly after I moved to Arlington, desperate for some help. Obviously, I was not ready for this however; I did meet another girl my age that had been widowed. We both felt the same way about the group. "How could all of these other people possibly know our pain?" I was sorry that someone's grandmother, mother or cousin had passed, but to me, my pain was so much worse. I had a hard time listening to the other people without wanting to scream at them and say "You think you have it bad, what about me? Can't you see that I am pregnant and widowed? No pain of yours can compare to my heartache." I was angry that these other people couldn't relate to my pain.

I also resented divorced people comparing their loss to mine. In a divorce, someone has a choice for his or her actions. Someone chooses that they are unfaithful, someone chooses drugs, someone chooses that they want out of the marriage. This is not the case in a death. I had no choice in John dying. No one came up to me as I was holding my dead husband's hand and said, "Excuse me…would you like to try to work things out with him…maybe some counseling would salvage this relationship?" I did not like John's death being compared to someone's divorce because neither of us had a choice in his death. Besides that, in a divorce, most children get to "keep" their Daddy; mine don't. All they have is me, and I am responsible for my children all of the time. I don't get a break every other weekend or for two to four weeks during the summer. Fortunately for me, gracious family and friends helped to provide some relief.

As I said, I wasn't angry at God, but I sure did question him. "Why me, God?" I'd see families in the store and wonder why they were so lucky to have each other. One week after John died, I was in the bank trying to deal with adjusting my bank accounts, when I spotted a young couple with a new baby. I thought to myself "Why was he able to be here for his child's birth when John won't? Why can't I have my husband? Why can't my children have their daddy? Why will my daughter never get to feel her daddy's gentle touch? WHY, WHY, WHY??!!!"

In addition, it is very common for widowed people to want to blame someone for their spouse's death. I felt someone had to be responsible for this tragic death. Lawsuits are very common. I personally filed a lawsuit against the Westin Corporation in the United States. I felt the Westin Hotel in Mexico was responsible for encouraging us to go to Lover's Beach. I asked for the best place to snorkel and the concierge answered, "You have to go to Lover's Beach. It is beautiful." One of the people from our group specifically asked, "Is it safe?" She said, "Oh yes, it is safe."

How could she tell us to go to this beach that is known to the locals as "Divorce Beach?" The locals call it this because if their spouse goes to that beach they will divorce them because it is so dangerous. There was also a death the week before at this beach, not to mention a tropical depression in the waters, which was unknown to all of us. Before tourism, this beach had a big billboard warning people to not go within one hundred feet of the water, but once tourism invaded Cabo, they took down the sign for fear of scaring off the tourists. On an average, one person a week drowns at this beach. They call this safe????

One of the reasons I went on this trip was because we were staying at an "American" owned hotel, or so I thought at the time. Once the lawsuit was filed, they claimed that the Westin in Mexico was a subsidiary of theirs even though out of the 30,000,000 shares, the Westin and Westin North America in the United States owns 29,999,996 of those shares. Because of all the legal red tape, it took over five years to settle the lawsuit. I filed the lawsuit to make a difference. Since the lawsuit was filed, the billboard warning people to not go within one hundred yards of the water is supposedly back in place and the American Consulate put a warning in the tourist paper shortly after John's death.

Whether it be a hotel, hospital, car manufacturer, restaurant or whatever, as a grieving person, blame is very common. In my case, I felt it was negligence on the hotel's part. Whether it was improper training or misinformation on their part, the hotel had the responsibility to keep their guests safe. Leading us to treacherous waters, without warning is not responsible behavior. My husband was not engaging in dangerous behavior when he died. He was merely walking along the shoreline of a so-called "safe place."

Chapter Two

Losses/Fears

Matthew 6:34 Therefore do not worry about tomorrow, for tomorrow will worry about itself. Each day has enough trouble of its own.

The losses I experienced when John died were innumerable. There was the loss of his love, support, laughter, intelligence, comfort and so many other things that made him so very special to me. Then, I realized that I was not going to be growing old with him. I felt like I had lost my whole future. I hadn't ever imagined my life without him in it. Now, that was my life.

My losses included the loss of a father to my children. Thinking that no one would ever love my children like John did. I lost my lover and best friend. I had the loss of not having someone to take care of us financially. I now had burdens that I never had before and they were all on one person…me! Talk about a career change!

I missed cooking for him. I missed not being able to share what Brandon did while he was gone. I missed the physical presence, his body, his clothes, sleeping next to a warm body, his smell. I think I must have slept with the same sheets on my bed for over a month, because his scent still lingered. I'd wrap myself in his robe to smell his scent. I thought if I could smell him then he was still with me.

I didn't like going through the men's department. It depressed me to know that I didn't have a special someone to dress. "Would I be alone the rest of my life?" I couldn't imagine not ever loving again, but the thought of it ever happening again seemed remote. John wasn't perfect and neither was I, but I felt we were perfect for each other. I didn't think I would ever be able to find that again, nor could I even fathom having another relationship with any other man.

With John's death came fear, which can really take charge of your life if you let it. One of my biggest worries was for my children. I worried about Brandon. I wondered how this would affect his life. Would he grow up normal? I was concerned about this baby inside of me. How would I tell her about her daddy? Would she ever get to know what it is like to be a daddy's girl? I had so many questions, but no one to answer them. I wanted to meet someone like me who had survived this and gone on with her life. Was that even possible?

Most widows' biggest fear is money. Mine was. Even though there seemed to be enough money to meet my needs, I still worried that I would not be able to provide for the children like John and I had planned. It did not seem like there would ever be enough money for that. I had a lot of people telling me what I needed to do, though. I had an appointment at the social security office two weeks after John's death so that I could start receiving death benefits as quickly as possible. I had no idea that I could qualify for social security. I thought that was only for retirement. The reason I had to wait two weeks for my appointment was because I had to provide them with an American death certificate, since the one I had was in Spanish from Mexico. There was a lot of red tape to sort through with John's death being in a foreign country.

In addition, I could not receive any of the life insurance benefits until they did an investigation of his death. This was the company's protocol since his policy had been in force for less then six months. They had to conduct a complete investigation. The agent kept apologizing to me. He did not want to have to do it, but knew it was necessary in order for me to receive the benefits. My life felt like such a mess!!

Financially had I not been where I was and not had the support of my parents, I probably would have been looking for someone to "save" me from this big mess. I just wanted someone to "takeover" my life so I wouldn't have so many responsibilities. Fortunately, I did have the support I needed and did not act on these feelings. It is so very important to not act on these feelings, because they *are temporary*. They will pass. I am glad that I did not succumb to these impulses otherwise; today I would probably be in a marriage that was made for the wrong reasons. I needed to focus on what my life was now. I had to get in touch with my strengths and search for what I had to offer others. This was not an easy task for me. I thought to myself, "What do I have to offer others? I am a single mom with two young children. Who is going to want me in their lives?" With time, I was able to get beyond these thoughts because I knew that I did have a lot to offer someone despite my status as a single mom.

Fear will never leave you if you let it stay. It will paralyze you to not move forward with your life. I do not fear death now that is has come so close to me. I would hate to think of not being able to see my children grow up, but if that is part of God's plan for my life than that is how it will be for us. I pray that I am able to see my children grow. I do not want them to be orphaned, but I also know that our three lives are not in my hands. All I can do is live day-to-day and not worry about the "what ifs" of life.

Having to bury the dreams of what might have been was very difficult. My life that was supposed to happen was cruelly and unjustly taken away from me. However, once I confronted this loss, I almost felt as if I had "permission" to move on with my life. Once I could do this, I knew that there was an empty spot next to me that would one day be filled by a very special person. I knew that I would love again and create with someone else and my children, a new life.

Chapter Three

Family

Deuteronomy 10:18 He defends the cause of the fatherless and the widow

Children

I am forever grateful for my children. They were the light in my life when everything seemed so dark. Brandon got me out of bed in the morning and Danielle kept me fed. I had to eat and sleep because of the little life that was left inside of me. I came to believe that my being pregnant was a coping mechanism that God gave me. I looked at my children and I saw hope for a future filled with love. Loving my children helped me to heal. My love for my children kept me from searching for someone to "save" me from all of my troubles.

John's death did not take away the love I had for him or the love he had for me. Our love for each other is evident in our children. They are products of our love. In our children, we are joined as one. I see John daily in my children. Before Danielle was born, I knew she was going to look like John and she does. Brandon has his smile and personality. That is how John lives on through his children.

Since Brandon had just turned two, his concept of death was very limited. Right after we moved in with my parents, he said, "Going bye-bye, want to see daddy." He then paused and said, "Daddy's in Heaven. Can't see daddy." I think he realized that John was not coming home. I told him, "Heaven is not a place we can go visit. Once a person dies and goes to Heaven, we don't see them again until God is ready for us." It was hard to tell what was going through my son's two-year-old mind. He cried more often and was clingy. This had to be confusing to him. John had been such a loving father to him and all of the sudden he was no longer in his life.

I was honest with Brandon about John's death from the very beginning. I tried to explain things as simple as I could. I told him, "Daddy was walking along the ocean when a big wave swept him in the water. Even though daddy was a good swimmer, he swallowed a lot of water which made his body stop working and he died." I went on and told him, "People usually don't die until they are really, really, old and mommy wants to live a very long time so I can see you and your sister grow big." I wanted to reassure him that I was here for him and wanted to be here for him and his sister.

I had read about "play therapy". Basically, the children act out their feelings with props. I bought him a dollhouse with all of the different family members to see if this "play therapy" would work. My hopes were that he would use it to act out his feelings. Of course, he wasn't the least bit interested in it. I had also read something about art therapy. From what I remember, children use certain colors to express their emotions. Red, brown and black represented anger. After reading this, I went back through this one coloring book that Brandon had been using. Every picture in the book was red, brown, or black, mostly black. I guess he was expressing his anger without me even knowing it. I was just glad he wasn't physically acting out his anger. That would have been too much for me to deal with at the time.

Every night before bed, we would read excerpts from two books. One was "Lets Talk about Heaven," by Debbie Anderson and "Someone I loved Died," by Christine Harder Tangvald. These books were above his age level, so I had to adapt them for his age. We would kiss a picture of mommy and daddy and tell daddy we loved him. After that I would ask him where his daddy was. He would say, "Heaven." After we would read the books, I would ask him who was someone that he loved that had died and he would answer, "Daddy."

Sometimes this nighttime ritual was too much for me emotionally. I will never forget the night that I was reading "Someone I Loved Died" and broke down crying. I couldn't go on reading it. I cried, "Mommy is so sad Brandon. I miss your daddy." He sat up in his bed and said, "It's okay mommy" and then sang, "Jesus' Love is Bubbling Over" to me. I had never heard this song, but I knew God was speaking to me through him to let me know His son, Jesus, loved me and would take care of me. That was the comfort I needed.

I would also tell Brandon that he was a very special boy because he had two fathers in Heaven, God and his daddy. I told him that there were not many children who could say that they had two fathers in Heaven, like he and Danielle. This came up in a children's church service. The woman doing the service started talking to the children about their "Daddy in Heaven." Brandon kept saying, "My daddy is in Heaven." The woman did not hear him say this, but I did. I knew it had to be confusing, so this is when I told him about having two fathers in Heaven.

Although my heart ached for Brandon not having his father, I also knew that this was a time I was going to have to set boundaries for him. It would have been easy to let him do whatever he wanted because I felt sorry for him, but I knew I wouldn't be doing him any favors later on in life if I let that happen. I did not want to have a child who was selfish and self-centered and thought the world "owed" him something because his father had died. I enforced rules and time-out when he disobeyed.

Having to enroll Brandon in a Mother's Day Out program two months after John's death was not something I wanted to do, but deep down I knew I needed to do it. I did not want to part with him. He was all that I physically had left of John. However, I knew that it was not emotionally healthy for him not to be around other children. If I didn't take this stand, once Danielle was born, I would have had problems. It was heart wrenching when I had to pull him off of my leg as I left him that first day. The director of the program was a good family friend, so I felt very comfortable putting him in this program. I knew his teacher was a good strong Christian who was praying for us. Despite the rocky first few weeks, we both adapted and the tears eventually stopped as I dropped him off for the day. He loved his teacher and his new friends.

Because Brandon would hear me call my parents "mom and dad," he started calling them "mom and dad" also. It only took one time of me hearing him call my mom "mom" to change my way of addressing my parents. They went from being called "mom and dad" to "Grandma and Grandpa." It became such a habit that to this day I still call them "Grandma and Grandpa."

As Brandon got older, he yearned for a father in his life. One year later, when he was three, we were moving into our new house. He said, "Now that we are getting a new house are we getting a new dog and new daddy?" I told him, "No, getting a new house did not come with a new dog and new daddy."

Children think in simple terms unlike us. One year later, at the age of four he still had a similar idea.

This time, the topic came about at breakfast after I had made some biscuits. Brandon said, "Did daddy like these biscuits we are eating?" I told him that I didn't know since he never had these biscuits when he was alive. He then continued to say, "We have two empty seats at the table. One is for our step-daddy and one is for our daddy." I told him, "Remember, your daddy that helped you be born died and is in Heaven." Brandon said he knew that, but he was talking about his new daddy. I said, "I know this is confusing, but when mommy meets a man that will be her husband, he would be his step-daddy and I couldn't have two husbands, only one." Then he said, "When you find that special man that God has picked out for us, I want him to be my daddy and I think his name will be John. You can pick him out of one hundred men." I asked him where I might find these one hundred men and he said, "At the store, the man store." So, one year later, at the age of four, Brandon thought we could go shopping for a new daddy.

Also as Brandon got older, he started to ask more perceptive questions. Another night I will never forget with him was when we were reading the story of Jonah. He asked, "Why didn't God send a big fish to save daddy?" I honestly told him, "Brandon, I don't know." "I don't know" came out of my mouth quite a bit and still does regarding John's death. Brandon even asked "Why did those other men make it out of the water and daddy didn't?" Again, my response was, "I don't know Brandon, but one other man besides your daddy died and we don't know why they couldn't make it out of the water. I just don't know."

For the longest time, I tried to convince myself that Brandon would remember his daddy. Brandon has an amazing memory. I was so sure that this was a gift from God so that he would remember John. However, three years later I had to finally accept that he had no recollection of his father other than what I told him or pictures he saw. This was brought to my attention when we were in the car one day. I heard a song that reminded me of John and told Brandon the song reminded me of his daddy. Brandon then said, "Was my daddy nice?" I told him "Yea, your daddy, was a nice guy, you would have really liked him." Then Brandon said, "Yea, but I was in your tummy when he died, so I didn't get to know him." I told him, "No, Danielle was in mommy's tummy when daddy died. You were two years old, which is really young. You were too young to remember your daddy and that's okay. You can ask mommy or Nanny and Paw Paw about daddy. We can tell you whatever you need to know." He said, "I know." That was the end of the conversation. However, this conversation made me realize how unrealistic it was for me to expect a child of twenty-five months to remember his father no matter how amazing his memory is.

I have tried very hard to make sure that he does all of the "boy" things in life. He started soccer and baseball at four. Soccer wasn't a hard sport for him with me because I played when I was younger, but baseball was more of a challenge. One of his first baseball practices has been ingrained in my head. I showed up to his practice and most of the dads were there to help. The boy that was paired up with Brandon wasn't throwing the ball to him. The dad asked why he wasn't playing catch. In a bratty tone, the boy said, "He doesn't know how to throw." I don't think it fazed Brandon that the boy said this, but my eyes filled up with tears. I wanted to go over to that little boy and say, "No, he doesn't know how to throw a baseball. His dad is dead. He doesn't have a daddy like you to teach him." Despite this one episode with t-ball, I was very fortunate to have loving coaches who made the extra effort with Brandon.

Whether John realized it or not, Danielle was his good-bye gift to me. When I lost the life of John, I gained the life of Danielle. She was what gave me life at a time in my life that I really didn't want to go on living. John left behind the two lives of Brandon and Danielle, which were my saving grace. God blessed me with a beautiful and healthy daughter. I could not see the beauty of it at the time of her birth, but now I do. God gave me an awesome gift of life. I couldn't have asked for a better parting gift from John. I might not have had Danielle's earthly father present for her birth, but her Heavenly Father was and is still present in our lives.

Every night after John's death, I prayed that God give me a sign that John would see Danielle. At first, I prayed that he would be present in the delivery room. I just knew when she was born that I was going to see a bright light shining down on her at her birth. Unfortunately, the only bright lights I saw were the floodlights the doctor had shining down on me. I am sure there was a presence in the room when she was born, but not one that I could physically see.

After Danielle's birth, I kept praying for God to send me a sign that John had seen his beautiful baby girl. Again, I thought I would wake up in the middle of the night and see him standing over her bassinet. I kept her in her bassinet as long as I could, clinging to that hope. The day came when I finally moved her to the crib, never having seen the vision I expected. I still continued to pray for my sign.

Finally, God answered my prayers better than I could have imagined! I had Danielle's baptism eight months after John's death on what would have been our fourth wedding anniversary. The day after the baptism, my sister-in-law, Sonia, took some pictures of Danielle and me outside the house. When she got the pictures developed, she called all excited. One particular picture of Danielle and I had a beam of light shining down over our heads. The frame before the picture showed that there was nothing that could have caused that kind of reflection. At first, I was skeptical, but I now know that was a true gift from God. If I look closely enough at the picture I can see a little boys' face. I say that is our guardian angel letting us know that John has indeed seen his little girl. What a wonderful way to have my prayers answered.

Part of the reason this was so special has to do with a poem that was written for us and given to us the day of John's funeral. One of my in-law's neighbor's daughter, who was also pregnant and due around the same time as I, wrote it. Her name is Brandi Ponson and she wrote this following poem:

In Your Time of Sorrow

I know there's nothing in the world that anyone can say
To make tonight and tomorrow better in any possible way.

It's going to be so difficult especially the next few days
To see a "bright side" will be hard when so many dark are
in the way.

I'm sure it seems as though that you will never make it
through
You have so many feelings; You wonder what to do.

You're feeling so much pain; You ask the reason "why?"
He had so much to live for and all you can do is cry.

I feel that even though I knew John only as a man

*That God is letting him send these words to your heart right
through my hands.*

*He loves you all so very much; He's sorry he had to go
God needed him in Heaven to watch you as you grow.*

*He will keep you all safe; He will watch over you forever
He'll be your angel in the sky and will never leave you ever.*

*He'll be with you always deep down in your heart
He'll live in your soul forever; You'll never be far apart.*

*He says that when you feel the warmth of the sun so very
bright
To know that it is him and that you're never out of sight.*

Note the last stanza and you can see why that picture meant
so much to me.

When it came to dealing with her father's death, it was much
different for Danielle than Brandon. She has not had a father
present in her life. She knows no other life than what she has.
One day, she told the pizza delivery guy, "My daddy died in the
ocean." He kind of looked at her and then at my mom to see if
he heard her right. My mom told him, "Yes, her daddy died in
the ocean." I felt sorry for that delivery guy. He was saying he
was really sorry to hear that. Danielle will tell whoever and
whenever. You never know when it will come out of her mouth.
To Danielle, death is a very ordinary and simple thing. If only
we as adults could think on these same terms about death.

Brandon looks just like me. There is no doubt he is my child,
but Danielle doesn't. She looks much more like her father than

me. Because of this, I would encounter remarks such as, "She must look just like her daddy" or "I bet she is a daddy's girl." Of course, either she or Brandon would be quick to tell that innocent stranger that their daddy had died and I would have to assure the person that they were telling the truth. I felt the need to clarify how long it had been and we were doing okay now.

Danielle also had a similar notion that when she gets a new daddy that his name will be John. I have had to explain the same things to her that I had to explain to Brandon at the age of three. I reiterated that his name probably wouldn't be John, but he would be very special and very lucky to have us in his life. She would say, "I know."

Like Brandon, Danielle at the age of three was also ready for her mommy to get married. The only difference was that she also wanted a baby brother and sister. She informed my boyfriend that she wanted a baby brother and sister. He told her that I needed to be married to have a baby and she said, "I know, I want you to marry my mommy." She was very vocal about wanting a daddy along with a baby brother and sister. She would tell her teacher and friends at school that her mommy was having a baby. When this got back to me, I had to inform her that mommy wasn't having a baby and that I needed to be married before I could have a baby. She said, "I know, I didn't' say you were going to have a baby now, but one day."

At the age of four, she still wanted a daddy, but it was at a different level. At this age, she seemed to be starting to search for her identity. She would ask more questions about John. She has a heart locket with a picture of John and I in it. She would wear it to school to show her friends that she also had a daddy. She wanted to be like all of her other friends who had a mommy and daddy.

I have taken all of our photos of John and memorabilia of

John and put them in an antique chest. Both children know it is there for them to look at whenever they want. Brandon has not shown any interest in it, but Danielle does. She will ask to take out and look at photos of "John." When she was four, she would ask if she could take the pictures to school to show her friends. This would make me sad, because I knew how much she wanted a daddy in her life and this was causing a void in her life by not having a father.

To fill this void, she was drawn to males. At times, it was quite embarrassing to me. One time, at Burger King, a man in line in front of us started talking to her. She reached out her arms for him to pick her up in his arms. After we sat down, I tried to explain to her, we don't do that with strangers. Most men will respond, "She sure is a friendly little girl." She is friendly and it bothers me that she is so friendly with men, especially men she doesn't know very well. She used to hop on a man's lap before a woman's. I thought that my dad's presence in her life would be a substitute for not having a father, but it wasn't. My dad used to travel during the week and was only home on the weekends, which wasn't enough.

In addition to my dad's presence, when Danielle was two, I had my first serious relationship. I thought that this would make a difference, but she was still drawn to men, even though he was a big part of our lives. To me, she seemed to get plenty of male attention, but for some reason she wanted more. I continued to reiterate that she needed to talk to me before she goes to a stranger, sits on a strangers lap, or hugs or kisses someone, even if it is mommy's friend.

One of the women from the support group I ran, shared with me how her two year old daughter was so drawn to men it embarrassed her. At that time, I didn't think much of that remark because Danielle was still a baby, but it stuck with me.

I'm glad she shared that with me, because it helped me to know that this was a "normal" response for her. Danielle is a very loving child. I don't want her to lose that gift, but I want her to exercise more caution. I thought that raising a son without a father would be more of a challenge for me, but it turned out to be quite the opposite. This was all new territory for me, since I hadn't gone through this with Brandon.

Parents

Moving back home with my mom and dad felt like a step backward for me in my life. I felt "inadequate" by not being able to take care of my family and myself. When I moved back home with my parents, I went back to being their "daughter." Actually, I went back to being their "little girl." I know that no matter how old Brandon and Danielle are that they will always be my babies. I also know how it feels to see your children hurting and being unable to make them feel better. I hid a lot of my emotions from my parents because I didn't want them to have to suffer any more than they were already. I needed them to be strong for my children. I was afraid that if I shared my sorrow with them it would prevent them from providing that strength.

I'm not sure that I did the right thing by not sharing my grief with them. I didn't want to be any more of a burden to them. I think that I would probably deal with it differently if I were to experience this type of pain again. They could not understand my heartache unless I shared it with them. I could not expect my mom and dad to understand all of my anguish since I kept it inside and put up a "strong" front for them.

I do not know what I would have done without my parents. They took care of Brandon and me those first few months when

I wasn't capable of doing so. They were exactly what I needed for those first few months after Danielle's birth. My mom was available to help take care of Brandon when I wasn't capable. It was hard enough for me to pull myself out of bed every day. Feeding and dressing Brandon wasn't always a priority. My mom was there to provide a routine and normalcy in his life. I didn't feel like I had a normal life, but my mother and father made him feel like he did. Now, of course, both of my children feel and do have normal lives. It is all how we choose to view our lives. If we choose to see our lives as "abnormal," then that is how it will seem. I didn't want my children to see themselves any different than anyone else. They are not different. They still have a loving family. Some children with both parents in their lives don't have that, but we do.

It is hard to believe that my dad was in the delivery room with me when Danielle was born. He wasn't even in the delivery room when I was born. That experience was a real eye opener for him. But also, I think it formed a unique bond between he and Danielle. My mother has a special bond with my children too. She sees my children as her own children since she is so close to them. I am thankful for my parents and for their health. They are able to do things with my children that they were unable to do with my brothers and me when we were younger.

Not many people in my situation have the opportunity to have both parents take them into their home to support them and their children. Divorce is so common in this day and age; that to have both parents still married after all these years was a blessing for me. Again, God was continually providing for my children and I. I was in a stable and secure environment for all of us. My children were able to witness a loving relationship between husband and wife that I couldn't provide for them at that time. They have a special connection with their grandparents. Again, I do not know what I would have done without all of their love and support for all of us.

When I first moved in with my parents, they wanted to take care of us for however long they needed. They were going to sell their house and buy a bigger house that could accommodate both of our families. We had contacted a realtor and began the house hunting process. Then, one weekend, my mom and dad went out of town leaving Brandon and I alone. I thought to myself, "This is really nice having time to ourselves. I'm not sure I want to live with mom and dad forever." That afternoon as I was driving to a support group meeting, I noticed the land behind my parents' house. A developer had come in about six months prior to John's death and subdivided the land behind their house into eight lots. There were two lots for sale that backed up to my mom and dad's backyard. I had this brainstorm, "Why not buy the lot behind them and build a house with a gate to their backyard?"

Because of this feeling of independence, I knew there would eventually come a time when I would want to move out and be on my own. When my parents got back into town, I suggested this proposal to them. My dad said, "That's the best idea yet." My mom and dad didn't want to sell their house and take on a house payment, but they were willing to do whatever they needed to take care of the children and me. I bought one lot and my dad bought the other hoping that my brother, Vince, and his family would eventually move back to town and build a home next door to me.

It took eight months for me to sell my house in Henderson. The building of my new house was contingent upon the sale of this house. As soon as I closed on the Henderson house, I broke ground for my new home behind my parents. My life was finally coming together. I was literally building my new life and moving forward. Even though I made house payments on the house in Henderson for eight months (having never lived in it), I knew it would sell when the time was right. By the time it was built, I was ready for the transition. It all happened in God's time, not mine. I wanted the house to sell sooner, but God knew when I was ready to move into my own house, not me.

Living with my parents is what I needed that first year. However, I knew I was going to eventually need to start taking responsibility for my children and myself. This was scary for me, since I had never done this before in my life. I had an easy life with mom and dad. I didn't have to cook or clean. My mom took care of us like we were all three her children. Because my mom took care of these things, I was able to learn how to handle our finances. When it was time to move, I had gained the confidence to be able to do this on my own.

Building the house behind my mom and dad's made me feel secure. Our backyards are touching. There is even a gate to go through one backyard to another. They have the swimming pool, so we have access to it, but I don't have that extra responsibility of maintaining a pool. My children think it is pretty neat to be able to walk over to Grandma and Grandpa's house.

In-laws

My relationship with my in-laws has been a challenging one. We have all had to deal with intense grief, so it was difficult for any of us to see beyond our own unique grief. I knew that I was hurting in my own way and that my mother-in-law and father-in-law were hurting in a different way. I knew that they could not possibly know what I was feeling because they still had each other and they had each other to raise all of their children together. But, I also didn't know what they were feeling because both of my children were alive. However, as I have learned, no one can predict life and I could one day experience their pain.

Early on there was quite a bit of tension between my mother-in-law and me. I tried to help her with her grief, but instead was frustrated and confused with our relationship. I felt like she resented me and didn't want to be around me because I was a reminder of what had happened. I prayed about it continually. Finally, God gave me the answer through a dream. Since John's death, I have only had three dreams with him in it and this was one of them.

In this particular dream, he was in a hospital on life support. I had just had a confrontation with his mother. I ran into the hospital room crying to John and begging him for his help. There was a breathing tube in his mouth. All of the sudden the other end of the tube was in my hand so I put it to my ear. When I did, I heard him say, "I love you." When I realized that he could hear me I cried, "John, what can I do about your mother?" The tube, still in my hand was brought to my ear and he said, "Nothing."

It took that dream for me to realize that he was right. There was nothing I could do to help his mother. She had to help herself and work through the grief without me. I listened to God and quit trying. Once I did that, our relationship improved. The stress from early on seemed to build a wall between us, which has caused our relationship to be a bit strained.

When John first died, I thought for sure we would see his parents all of the time and they would be a big part of our life, but it was too hard for all of us. Neither of us wanted to make the extra effort to go see each other. I felt like they should come see us, since I was the one with two young children who would have to drive five hours alone to go see them. They probably thought I should make the effort and not them. I saw things my way and they saw things their way. That doesn't make either one of us right or wrong. That just makes us human.

There will always be times when things may be awkward, but that is true with all relationships in life. It took both of us realizing that each of us had a different pain that the other couldn't possibly understand. This wasn't a competition for who hurt worse. We all hurt in our own way. Each person takes his or her own time to work through grief. There is no time limit on grief. We all handle it differently and at a different pace. Just because someone doesn't handle their grief just like me doesn't mean their way is wrong.

Not only from my own experience, but also from others in the widowed support group, I have found similar situations with in-laws. From the support group I learned that widowed people have either a fantastic relationship with their in-laws, a strained relationship, or sometimes no relationship. It saddens me that some people opt for no relationship. The emotions are high and things are said and done that won't be forgiven.

I know that at times it has been difficult for me, but I have never severed those ties. As my life goes on it is more difficult to be as close to them as I would like due to the "busyness" of our lives. However it is like that in all of my relationships, not just with them. We have sports and activities every weekend, which makes it difficult to see them on regular basis. I am just thankful that they are a part of our lives.

Chapter Four

People Mean Well, But Don't Take Everything They Say Literally

Deuteronomy 7:9 Know therefore that the LORD your God is God; he is the faithful God.

As a result of John's death, I am more attune to people's insincerity. I can tell if someone is really sincere in what they are saying. It is something that I can feel. When someone says, "You are in my prayers," I can tell if it is really happening or something they are saying because they think it is the "right" thing to say to me.

It perturbed me when people would say, "Lisa lost her husband." I had one person say, "Lisa lost her husband in Mexico." I wanted to scream, "He is not lost! He is dead!!!" John was not lost somewhere wandering the beaches of Mexico. John was dead. I would politely correct someone by saying, "My husband died while we were in Mexico."

I got tired of everyone asking, "How are you?" Did they really want to know that I had a horrible day? Or that I had a hard time getting out of bed in the morning and making it out the front door? I didn't want anyone's pity, so I would usually answer, "I'm fine" with a fake smile on my face. Asking the question, "How are you?" is too vague. I ask my newly widowed friends, "How are you today?"

Hearing all of the trite sayings got tiresome. People would say, "God wouldn't give you more than you could handle," "It was God's will" or "It was his time." I didn't buy or accept any of those clichés. A loving God would not do this to one of His children. He would not purposely inflict this kind of pain upon me. We live in an imperfect world, where bad things happen to good people. Some might say, "God is sovereign, so why didn't He intervene?" My response to that is, "How many other times did God intervene to save John's life that I don't know about. Am I going to hold it against him that this one time he didn't?" For John's age I feel like he had a long full life. According to *Psalm 139:16, All the days ordained for me were written in your book before one of them came to be.* It is a comfort to read this scripture and know that God had plans for John and a long life wasn't in those plans.

Right after John's death, I had many people rallying around me with their love and support. Eventually these family and friends returned to their normal lives, while I as left to pick up the pieces of my now shattered life. I now had to begin a new life by myself. These people meant well when they said they would never forget us, but they did. They got bogged down with their own lives. They cared and had good intentions, but it felt like they didn't care enough to follow-up and periodically check on me to see how I was doing. They saw how "well" I had coped in those early days and assumed I was "okay."

I had other friends say and offer things, yet never follow through with them. This was very disappointing for me. I thought they were sincere in what they had told me and never expected them to "disappear" from our lives. When these friends "forgot" about us, I realized now that John was gone, we were no longer going to be a part of their lives. My biggest complaint about these people was that they gave me false hope. I really believed that they would do all of the grandeur things they promised. They might have been able to "forget" what they said, but I didn't. I felt alone and abandoned by these "friends."

I know that it is a two way street. I understand that these people might not have known what to say to me. Because of this, I would send notes along with photos of the children and not have them acknowledged. I felt as if my reaching out was insignificant and that I was now meaningless to them since John was not here. When these things happened, it reinforced my feelings of abandonment. I tried to make excuses for these people. One excuse was, "Maybe they are embarrassed to call now since it has been so long since they had spoken to me." Or I thought maybe they were really busy with their jobs and children… but I finally realized that there were no excuses. One phone call was all it would have taken to lift my spirit.

About two years after John's death, one of his high school buddies called from out of the blue. Apparently, he and his wife were in town for a wedding and wanted to get together with us. It made my day when he called. It was very special to have one of John's best friends and his wife spend time with us. John's friends are a link to John's past. These people know parts of John that I never knew. I will never forget his kind gesture. He is still good at keeping in touch with me. He and his wife named their first son, Caleb John. They chose "John" as his middle name in memory of "My John." What an honor and tribute.

I implore friends and family to keep in touch with the widow/widower even if the spouse was their friend. These people who made the extra effort with me have no idea how much their phone call or note meant to me. I would usually get it on a day I needed it most. I cherished we had not been forgotten by these kind friends. To this day, I still get notes from many of John's friends. Many still send us our annual Christmas card. I look forward to these every year.

I soon realized that it was time for me to rewrite my address book. True to the notion that you find out who your real friends are when tragedy strikes. It seemed like most of John's friends were uncomfortable with just me. All of them were couples and I was not. Now that John was not in my life, neither were these friends. This was sad for me, but true. So, not only was there the loss of my husband I was dealing with, but also that of friends.

If I have learned one thing from John's death, it is you don't take your friends or family for granted. I was a single mom with two young children. Regardless of my burdens and responsibilities, I made it a point to remember my friends. Today and then, if someone is on my mind, I make a note of it so I will be sure to write, call, or email him or her. The sad thing for me was that when I needed some of these friends the most, they weren't available to me. This was a true test of who my "real friends" were in my life. Those friends who were there for me then are still here for me now. That is a true friend.

The best friends that I had in those early days of grief were the ones that talked less and listened more. I wanted to share my feelings without someone trying to explain or analyze them for me. One memorable talk I had was with a priest by the name of Father Mark. He came to see me the first week I was back in Arlington. He kept shaking his head in disbelief and he told me, "Lisa, I have no idea why this happened. It baffles me. I would have to argue with God about this. I don't understand this."

That was exactly what I wanted to hear. I didn't need to hear from clergy that this was "God's will." I needed to be reassured that this was inexplicable.

Chapter Five

Hope: Acceptance/Recovery
(There is a light at the end of the tunnel)

2 Samuel 22:29 You are my lamp, O Lord; the Lord turns my darkness into light.

Right after John's death, all I could see was pitch-black darkness. But, little by little, as I moved forward in life, I began to see the light. Once I could see a glimpse of light again, my life started to take shape. It was a relief to know that my life was important. I was a whole rather than a half! I needed to realize that just because John was not physically here with me didn't mean I wasn't a complete individual.

Once I was able to start moving forward in life, things seemed to get better for me. I finally got to a point where I could look beyond my own grief and reach out to others. I had to finally accept that I would never know the answers to all of the "why's?" in my life. I came to the point when I wondered, "Why not me? Why should God give me a life free of pain and suffering?" God never promised me a life without sorrow, but he has promised His faithfulness. Once I could see my life as it was and I was happy with it, than I had accepted the death and my new life. I was content being alone. I did not feel the initial emptiness and loneliness. I felt proud that I was a survivor…proud, not glad.

My reality was that I would never physically be with John again and all of our hopes and dreams together would never happen. However, I still had hopes and dreams of my own that could happen. My life won't ever be the same now that death has touched it. Everything has changed, including me. I came to this revelation when I realized that I could make a difference. I saw that it did matter that I was able to help other people through my tragedy. My hopes and dreams evolved from what I would have had in my married life with John to what I, Lisa, a single widowed mother of two young children could do to make a difference in other people's lives as a result of John's death.

My hopes and dreams included me having the strong desire to start a support group for other younger widowed people. I wanted to write this book along with a Christian children's book dealing with the death of a parent targeted for a preschooler. These were things that I desired to have that weren't available to me. I knew there had to be others like me, so that is why I pursued these new goals. Along with these, I still had the desire to one day date and remarry. It wasn't a priority, but I knew that I wanted to love again. These were now all of my hopes and dreams. I went from being hopeless to having a future. Life got better and better for me.

I have realized that I won't ever stop grieving. Grief has now become a part of my life that I am continually integrating into it. The best recovery for me has been a gradual recovery. I no longer see my grief as a tragedy, but as a divine gift. Because of my grief, I have a newfound appreciation for what is important. I can see that John's death has not been in vain. Good has come out of it. I chose to not get wrapped up in all of my sorrows. I chose to celebrate all of my blessings.

The true healing in my life took place when I could stop calling attention to my wounds. I focused on how I could grow from this and become a better person because of it. I focused on the saying, "Happiness doesn't come from without, it comes from within." This happened when I could be that light in someone's life that was experiencing those dark feelings that were once such a huge part of my life. The mourning and grieving for myself came to an end because I was willing to start new growth.

There are always going to be times in my life where I may experience those "waves" of grief, but those waves are now for other people. Current events tend to cause the emotions to resurface. For example, when the World Trade Center was bombed on September 11, 2001, my heart went out to those men and women who had lost a spouse and to the children who were now without one or both of their parents. I saw two different interviews with women who were pregnant. I was at the gym on the treadmill when I saw the first interview. My heart ached for this women as tears rolled down my face listening to her. Had I not been at the gym, I wouldn't have held back so much on my emotions. I had to keep from really crying.

The pain I feel now is for other people who are experiencing the same or similar loss as mine. I know their pain. I feel their pain. As I watch them on T.V. or read about these people in the paper, I know they are all still in shock. That is why it appears that they are coping so well. I know that once the real pain hits is when they will have a hard time. When emotions are high, there is help. Ellie Carey, past president of our WPS Chapter, says, "Once the casserole brigade is over, we are left alone." People do go on with their lives and our situation is no longer a focus for them. So, when I see or hear about people who are in similar circumstances as I was, my heart aches for them because I know what is ahead of them.

When should you take off your wedding ring??? This was a question I thought about quite a bit. When I would meet someone who had been widowed a while, that was one of the first questions I asked them. Once I could take my wedding ring off of my left hand, I was accepting my new status. In actuality, the wedding ring was a protective circle around my finger. As long as I was wearing it, I was "protecting" myself from being hurt again. I took my ring off in my own time, not anyone else's. However, I knew that as long as I was wearing it, I was not accepting my single status.

Each person handles this situation in his or her own way. There is no "right" or "wrong" way to deal with this. It is a very individual decision. Initially, I moved it from my left to right hand. I soon realized that regardless of which hand I wore my wedding ring; people still assumed I was married. Apparently, some people wear it on their right hand, depending on their culture or if they are left handed.

Eventually, I went back and forth on wearing my ring and not wearing my ring. Pretty soon I realized I wasn't wearing it anymore. Not wearing my ring was finally accepting my status. I was a single person, not married. That was a gradual process. When I was first widowed, I said I would never take off my wedding ring or have it reset…..NEVER!

Four years later, that never happened. I had my ring reset into a "Mother's Ring." My reason for not having it reset was so I could pass it on to Danielle just as I had received it. After four years of paying insurance premiums on a ring that wasn't being worn, I finally decided it was time to wear it. I reset it with my diamond in the center and the children's birthstones are on each side. It now signifies my life. The diamond in the center represents the union between John and I that produced my children, who are my life. Because of that diamond, I was given these two lives to celebrate. Now this is a ring that will have true meaning to my daughter.

Chapter Six

Choose Life!

*Isaiah 30:21 Whether you turn to the right or to the left, your
ears will hear a voice saying "This is the way; walk in it."*

When tragedy struck, I saw two choices before me. First, I
could wallow in self-pity, feel sorry for myself and blame all of
my problems on what had happened to us. My second choice
was to go on living. For me, that wasn't much of a choice.
Because I had children, I was obligated to lookout for their
welfare. If I became bitter and angry, then I would be fostering
that in my children. I knew as a mother that I had to surround my
children with love and the best role model possible—now that
I was the only one they had. This wasn't my choice to be a single
mom. It was forced upon me.

I learned that I couldn't focus on all of my losses; I had to
focus on all of my gains. My life was enriched. No, I didn't have
a spouse or a father to my children, but I did have my life and
many, many wonderful people in it. This may not have been
what I had planned, but I felt blessed to be alive and with my
children. If I didn't have that outlook on life, I would have and
would still be one unhappy woman.

I have also learned to let all the special people in my life know how much their love and friendship is valued. I now live for today and not always assume there will be a tomorrow because I now know some tomorrow's may never come. There are no second chances once that person is gone. I make sure the people I love know it. I cherish them. If I die tomorrow, I know my children will know how much I loved them. I have no regrets with John. He knew how much I loved him when he died.

Support

2 Corinthians 1:3-4 Praise be to the God and the Father our Lord Jesus Christ, the Father of Compassion and the God of all comfort, who comforts us in all of our troubles, so that we can comfort those in trouble with the comfort we ourselves have received from God.

I knew immediately after John's death that God was going to use my tragedy to help others in similar situations. The day before John's funeral, the Lord convicted me of this. I had this strong feeling about getting through this so I could help others. I told my family, "When I get through this, I am going to help other people in my situation." This was said right before the funeral. God spoke to me early on about an outreach ministry.

At first I thought I would go back to school and get a degree in Bereavement Counseling, but instead, God opened the doors for me to start a support group called Widowed and Young or WAY, hence the title of this book. Once I contacted Widowed Persons Services of Tarrant County, also called WPS, I knew this was an organization that would help me. I had no idea that they would be helping me start this new support group for young widows and widowers.

Widowed Persons Services is a national organization that was founded through AARP (American Association of Retired Persons) in 1973. It was formed with the concept that other widowed people are the best people to reach out and help others who have been recently widowed. All of the facilitators are not paid professionals, but volunteers who are widowed themselves. It is open to all widowed people regardless of their age, race or sex.

As I look back on my life, I see how God was preparing me for this. I received my undergraduate and graduate degree in Speech Communications, which emphasizes Public Speaking. I married two months after graduation and never found a job that utilized my communication skills. I felt as if my degree had been a waste. I used my degree more than I ever thought possible through Widowed Persons Service. No, I did not get paid to do support group meetings, but the rewards were worth more than any dollar figure. No paying job could have fulfilled me more than this. To see the progress of someone who first came to the support group distraught and without hope was worth all of my efforts.

Other widows/widowers are the best support system because they really do know how the other is feeling. The support group is a safe place to talk about your feelings. You can say your spouse's name without someone getting uncomfortable or changing the topic. It also doesn't offer any of those clichés that are heard from so many "well meaning" people such as. "You are so strong" or "You are such an inspiration." Even if these things were true, we still don't want to hear them.

Sometimes I would compare myself to an iceberg. Only a small part of my grief was seen above the surface, but what was really underneath it all? How much I hurt, how alone I now felt, how unjust my life was, how differently people now looked at me, and how hard it was for me to get a hold of each day. These are all feelings that other widowed people can help validate. A lot of people will say to widows/widowers that they aren't the same person. But, in our support group we know no other person than the one we have met. No one in the group has to worry about someone saying, "You just aren't your old self." No, we are no longer our "old self." How can we be now that our whole world has changed?

I met some very special friends through the WAY support group. When we would socialize it was quite unique. We could talk about death and sometimes find some "humor" in it. One time at dinner, there was a group of about fifteen of us. One of the men worked at a funeral home and the next thing you know we are talking about the price of caskets and the mark up on them. Only with another group of widowed people could we have this conversation and not be considered morbid. We could say what was on our minds without fearing what other people might think.

At the time I started WAY, Ellie Carey, was the president of Widowed Persons Service. When I first moved back home, she was the only person who I thought could understand what I was feeling. She was widowed the first time at the age of twenty-nine and left with two children—a one year old and a three year old. She understood my passion to get the WAY group started because there was not such a thing when she was widowed the first time. Because of her love, support and help, WAY was able to get launched approximately eight months after I approached her about it.

The words out of Ellie Carey's mouth regarding the membership cost of WPS are, "There are no fees to join. We have paid the highest price in life to be at this support group."

Since WPS is a nonprofit group, I had to find a free meeting place, free babysitting for those that might need it, and free speakers to talk to the group. I was not ready to facilitate the group for those first few months, so I enlisted the help of other widowed people to get us started with the meetings.

By taking the step to seek a support group, I was making a conscious choice to go on with my life. I encourage anyone in this situation to do the same. If there is not a support group for younger widows/widowers, start your own. God will open the doors for you if it is meant to happen. I love Helen Keller's quote, *"when one door of happiness closes, another opens, but often we look so long at the closed door that we do not see the one which has been opened for us."*

It took very little effort on my part to start the WAY group. I made a few phone calls and the wheels were in motion. I talked with a priest at a local church I had been attending. He offered the church without my asking. I then contacted WPS and told them we had a meeting place. Ellie Carey, helped me to round up facilitators for the first few months of meetings. Our first meeting was to take place approximately ten months after John's death.

One of the local papers came to my house and interviewed me for an article regarding the launch of WAY. My attitude was, "If only one person shows up at the meeting, then it was still worth the effort." I thought we might have five to ten people show up for that first meeting. Imagine my surprise when nearly forty people were jammed in the small room I had reserved! This was all the reassurance I needed to know I was doing the right thing. The support group started in March of 1996 and by that summer, Ellie Carey thought that I was ready to facilitate on my own.

Again, God had prepared me for this task by providing me with a degree in Speech Communications. I taught Public Speaking part-time on the college level before my son was born, so I was confident I could take on this role. I had talked about doing the support group, but never thought it would actually happen. I felt God's hand with the support. He opened the doors to make it possible, not me. I chose to walk through the door when the opportunity arose rather than slam it shut. Anyone could have done this support group; they probably ignored God's lead to let it happen. God led the WAY for me to start the group. That was why I chose the acronym WAY for Widowed and Young. *Matthew 7:7-8 Ask and it will be given to you; seek and you will find; knock and the door will be opened to you. For everyone who asks receives; he who seeks finds; and to him who knocks the door will be opened.*

I led and facilitated the WAY group for approximately two years. After that, I felt as if God was leading me in a different direction. Unfortunately, it is no longer active. WPS tried to keep it going, but it was hard to find someone my age to commit to doing it. It was a huge commitment on my part, but well worth it. I didn't have to pay a counselor $90 an hour when I could tell a room full of widowed people what I was feeling and experiencing. That was better than any therapy session I could have ever received.

Our support group would meet every other Friday. In February of 1997 one of our meetings happened to be on Valentine's Day. I remember driving to the meeting thinking, "How depressing is this? I am driving to facilitate a support group meeting on Valentine's Day." I shared this with the group and they all felt the same way. After our meeting, about 15-20 of us went to eat dinner. I had made reservations at a pizza place. I chose Friday evenings for our meetings because for many couples this is a "date night." I knew none of us were going on a date and being at the support group is better than sitting home alone feeling sorry for ourselves.

When we walked into the restaurant there were red and white balloons tied to all the chairs along with a reservation sign propped on the table that said "Young Widows Group." We all laughed because there were couples there on dates. I wonder what they thought about us? After dinner as we were leaving, we all took a balloon with us. When we went outside, all of us at the same time let go of our balloons and said "Happy Valentine's Day" along with our spouse's name. It was really neat. None of us there that night will ever forget this.

After about a year of meeting we even tried forming a social group for WAY. We called it YEA WAY for Young Energetic Adults Widowed and Young. We came up with the name at one of our group dinner socials. One of the guys said it should stand for "Young Energetic and Available." Then another one said, "It's time to get out of the WAY with YEA!" As you can see, the healing had begun with our whole group. There was about fifteen of us that would socialize on a regular basis. Our group was ready to move out of the support group, so that is how the social group evolved. We all kept in contact for about two years then eventually went our separate ways. It was time for all of us to move on with our lives.

Chapter Seven

Memories and Journaling

Philippians 1:3 I thank my God every time I remember you.

Memories are often painful, but not as painful as forgetting. There finally came a time for me when I could look past the agony of acute grief and remember happy times. When this happened, my memories became more comforting than painful. I thought that if I talked about John that I was living in the past. I now know that is not true. Recalling fond memories of John was not living in the past. My memories of John became my most important possession because it was all that I truly owned of him now that he was dead. The memories were all that remained of the relationship with John. Memories are one of the best legacies that exist after a spouse dies.

Personally, I could not surround myself with pictures of John. I didn't do that when he was alive, so it wasn't natural for me to do it when he was dead. I had a picture of John and I above Danielle's changing table. I finally had to put it away because it was too painful for me to see. Obviously, Danielle was oblivious to it, so there was no need to torture myself. I did have some guilt about not having his pictures everywhere. I felt like other people thought that I should, or that I was forgetting him by not having them around me.

Because of this guilt I felt, I was very creative on doing other things to preserve John's memory for the children. My brother, Vince, and his family had a star named after John. Along with this, they gave my son a telescope for Christmas so he can one day find his daddy's star. I have the constellation map for when he wants to do this. For Danielle, they gave her a heart shaped locket that has a star engraved on the outside and inside the locket is a picture of John and I together.

In addition to this, I wrote to a jeweler in South Texas by the name of Jeep Collins. He has a whole line of angels, crosses and other religious items. In his catalog, he has a short story that goes along with his charms. I was touched by this and wrote him a letter telling him about what had happened. I asked if he would make a custom order for us called "John's Angel" so that the children could always have their daddy close to their heart. He designed the "Protector Angel" for us. I never expected him to do this for a perfect stranger, but he did. I have the "Protector Angel" on a cross, pin, key chain, checkbook cover and charm.

Since I had young children, I also felt the need to commemorate John in a meaningful way for them. The best thing for them was to send balloons to Heaven on special days such as John's birthday, the day he died, and Christmas or any other time the children wanted to do it. I did learn from a widower friend of mine that if they want to attach a picture or note with their balloon to make sure they used Mylar balloons and lightweight paper. My friend learned the hard way, when his girls' balloons were dragging on the ground rather than flying to their mommy in Heaven. However, another member in the support group pointed out that Mylar balloons are not enviromentally friendly, so the alternative would be to use tracing paper with one or two regular balloons to lift their picture.

One of the most difficult things for me to do was part with John's belongings. I had to do it early on because of the move, but fortunately for me, my sister-in-law, Sonia told me to keep some of John's dress shirts so I could make the children quilts out of them. Not only did I have quilts made for each child out of these shirts, but I also recycled them into other treasures as well. I had teddy bears made that were clothed out of these shirts. For Christmas, I had small teddy bear ornaments made out of these shirt scraps. I gave them to family members to hang on their tree in memory of John every Christmas. Since John was a doctor, I also had boy angel dolls made that were clothed out of some of his scrub pants. The wings on them were from one of his lab coats.

I had a hard time parting with these shirt scraps, so I continued to have things made until they were gone. I had a Raggedy Ann doll made for my daughter. She is dressed in a patchwork dress with her bottoms made out of John's white lab coat. The woman who made it even put the pocket from the lab coat on Raggedy Ann's bloomers. Since I had this doll made for Danielle, I also had the same person make a small patchwork travel pillow for Brandon. She used some of the shirt pockets so Brandon would have some secret places to hide things. Brandon, at the age of nine still sleeps with that little pillow every night.

Out of the last shirt scraps, I had two smaller Raggedy Ann dolls made and some tooth fairy pillows. Danielle liked her big Raggedy Ann so much that she took it everywhere with her. Unfortunately, since she was only two when she got it, she took her outside to play and forgot her in the rain. Raggedy Ann now has "character." Her hair has been pulled along with the colors bleeding from the rain. She still loves her the same, but she didn't get the new one until she was a little older. I had the other doll made for my niece, Gianina, who was named after John and I. The apron on her is made from one of my shirts and the patchwork dress from John's shirts. This way she has a part of me and a part of John since she is named after the two of us. "Gianina" is the feminine form of John in Italian and her middle name "Marie" is my middle name.

For some reason, when John and I were married, I saved a pattern for a vest that was made out of shirt ties. I also saved twelve of John's ties that were my favorite. A close friend of mine made the vest for me. When I would facilitate the support group dealing with memories, I would wear this vest along with my Protector Angel pin. Again, this is something that will have meaning to my children. I had to get used to being the only one that remembered. Remembering the past is what made hoping for the future possible. I have the opportunity to help my children link their past and future.

Journaling was extremely therapeutic for me during that first year following John's death. It allowed me to express all of my feelings, thoughts and pain. Especially since I wasn't sharing them with my family. Journaling was an excellent vehicle for me to express what my life was like without John. Later, as I began to pick up the pieces of my life, my journal gave me a chance to see how far I had come. I often thought that I hadn't progressed in my grief or grown as a person, but then I would reread my journal and see that the good days were starting to outnumber the bad. Rereading my journal reminded me of this.

I chose my computer to journal. However, keeping a journal doesn't require this expense. All that is needed is a notebook, pen or pencil. When I started journaling, I made a commitment to myself to spend at least ten to fifteen minutes every day doing it. I soon found, that the words came so freely, that I usually spent more time than that on it each day. I looked forward to my journaling at the end of the day. However, as time went on, my journaling became less frequent, because I no longer needed it to express myself. I have included some excerpts from my journal to show the progress that I made.

July 5, 1995

...the hardest part of this loss is not just losing someone who you love dearly, but also the loss of our dreams and future. We were able to see the light at the end of the tunnel all during his residency....Now I don't see the light at the end of that tunnel. I know there is one, but it is not quite as bright as I had imagined. My faith in God is stronger than it has ever been.

September 17, 1995

Another hard day. I feel so sad and empty inside. I was able to make it to church....it is so difficult to see beyond my heartache on some days. I see all of these happy families and it doesn't seem fair that I am not one of them. I can't sleep tonight. I sobbed uncontrollably for about 15 minutes. I thought I was going to hyperventilate. I am so consumed with grief right now...I feel as if Danielle is also sobbing. It's probably just the hiccups, but I can't help but think that this must upset my unborn child.

October 16, 1995

Today marks exactly four months since John's death.

Usually I know when the 16th is here, but today I had to actually think about the day. Danielle has made such a difference in my life. She gives me so much peace. Maybe it is because I know that she is my last link to John.

December 16, 1996

It has been exactly six months since John's death. It is hard to believe it has been that long. At times, it seems as if time stands still. I don't feel as if I am moving forward or backward in time. It is hard to explain. Sometimes I still can't believe that I am here with my parents. I know that it has happened, but it is still so unbelievable.

April 1, 1996

I decided to take off my wedding ring. I didn't feel guilty about taking it off like I thought I would. It was almost a relief. I said I would **NEVER** take off my wedding ring, but I have. People still think I am married even thought I was wearing it on my right hand. I am tired of having to explain my situation.

June 14, 1996

It is hard to believe that last year on this day I was laying out by the pool in Cabo San Lucas, Mexico without a care in the world. I try not to think those thoughts too much today because they are really depressing. I try to think positive and look at how far I have come since June 16th of last year.

October 16, 1996

It has been so long since I have journaled. I just don't feel the need as much. I am so happy with my life and myself. I love my life and my children…what more can I ask for right now?

In addition to my journaling I also felt compelled to write a tribute letter after Danielle was born. This was my way of letting everyone know that I had a healthy little girl. So many people donated money for the children's future. I felt I owed them this letter. It was a way for me to express my feelings plus rejoice in my daughter's birth. I sent the following letter the week after Danielle was born. I had been compiling it for four months. I only shared this with a few close friends before I mailed it. Even my own parents didn't see it or read it until I was mailing it. It wasn't something I wanted to share until I mailed it.

Dear friends and family:

The past four months have been a trying time for me and my family, but due to the love and support of friends, family and the medical community, we are making it through these hard times. I will never get over John's death; however, I will make it through the grief. John was a very special person who touched many people's lives.

On October 11th, I had a healthy baby girl, Danielle Johnn Gardemal. She weighed 5 pounds and 12 ounces and measured 18 inches. John may not have been physically present for Danielle's birth, but I know in my heart that he was in the delivery room guiding the doctor's hands. He is our guardian angel watching over us. His spirit will live on forever in our children, Brandon and Danielle. They are his proud legacy. John gave me the two most precious gifts of life, for which I am forever grateful. The love that John and I shared will be eternally evident in our beautiful children.

Our love for John is larger than life itself. We have a bond with him that is eternal. John's life will always be with us. He lives on in our hearts, memories, and the lives of all those who knew him. We will all carry his specialness inside us in our memories now and forever.

At times the pain of losing John has been almost unbearable, however, the experience of loving and knowing him has been worth all the pain that I am enduring. I thank God for the time that I did get to spend with him. My love for John will never die.

We will never know why this tragedy happened. All I know is that God has other plans for John. John has gone before me with God to prepare a home in Heaven in which we shall both be together again when the time is right. It gives me peace to know that he will be waiting at Heaven's gate for me and our children with open arms.

God Bless

Even though I am not physically present, I am with you in spirit. –1 Corinthians 5:3

Over seven years later, it is still painful for me to read this letter. As time goes on, I forget how wretched with pain I was in those early months. Rereading this is a reminder of the intense grief I felt at one time. I chose writing this tribute letter to assist in my closure. This was also Danielle's birth announcement from me. Some people from the support group chose writing a good-bye letter for closure for some unresolved feelings. One person sent it up with a balloon; another burned it after they wrote it. Whatever you write, the Lord will lead you. As I reread my letter, I am amazed at the words in it. I don't remember writing this. I read it and think it is a beautiful letter, but also know that God had his hand on my hand as I wrote that letter. Those words are from God not me.

Chapter Eight

Second Year Struggles

Psalm 86:7 In my day of trouble I will call to you, for you will answer me

Part of the second year struggles is dealing with all of "the firsts." I knew for the one-year anniversary day of John's death I wanted to do something special. That was what John would have wanted for us all to do. He would have wanted us to celebrate his life and not mourn it. A celebration? It seemed odd that I tried so hard to make June 16th a special day. I thought of it as a day to celebrate. Was this demented? For me, it wasn't. Death is not the end of our being. Death was the beginning of John's eternal life. This was definitely a reason to celebrate our life now and the life we shared with John while he was here with us.

Since June 16th was John's "birthday in Heaven," I felt I needed to do something special to commemorate it. June 16th, 1996 was also Father's Day. We still had a lot of father's here with us to celebrate, not to mention our Father in Heaven that is always with us. I decided on having a Father's Day celebration at my parents' house for the occasion. I was still anxious about the day, not knowing what to expect, but I knew I would be surrounded with a lot of love to make the day easier on me.

On June 15th I went to a Jeep Collins Jewelry trunk show at one of the gift shops in town. I had written him a letter that previous fall requesting the "John's Angel." He responded in writing and said he would put it in his "idea" file. After, that I didn't think much about it. I thought he responded to my letter to be kind, but didn't think he would take any action. I went to the trunk show to thank him for taking the time to respond to my letter. I introduced myself to his wife and as soon as she heard my name she said, "John's Angel"…did he tell you he made it?" I told her, "No."

This was such a gift to receive this message the day before the one-year date. I knew that after hearing this that I was going to make it through June 16th and that it would be a good day. This was a message from God reassuring me about the next day. I was so overwhelmed by Jeep and Dana Collins kindness for a perfect stranger and at the same time amazed that they were so touched by my story to design the "Protector Angel."

When June 16th arrived, my whole family and close friends came together on this special day. I took my son and nephews to the store to pick out special balloons to send to John in Heaven with a message attached to them. It was a moving experience when the children let them go to John. My eyes filled with tears of joy. I was happy that we were all able to do this together and be together on this day. In addition, on this one-year anniversary, my sister-in-law, Sonia, had John's family write down their memories of John. She took these stories and compiled them in a book for the children. This was a priceless present.

The second year anniversary was "just another day." I woke up and didn't feel any different than any other day of my life. Two years ago on June 16th, it wasn't "just another day." This year it was. At 3:00 p.m., we did a balloon lift simultaneously with my niece and nephews in Chicago. Brandon and Danielle drew special pictures on tracing paper and we all said, "Happy Birthday Daddy." I continue to tell the children that June 16th is "Daddy's birthday in Heaven." The balloon lift was a tradition I wanted to continue every year as long as the children were willing. We did do it on the third anniversary, but by year four it dissipated. By the fourth year, that day slipped my mind and we didn't do anything special. I was reminded of the day when I received a card from an old friend that hadn't forgotten what happened. It was nice to know they still remembered.

By the second year when I would cry it was no longer for John, but for me…what I didn't have…where I was in life. I would cry because I was feeling sorry for myself versus before I would cry out in pain and anguish. For instance, when I had my first parent/teacher conference for Brandon. Of course, all the teacher could say about him were wonderful and great. After the conference, I got into my car and cried because there wasn't that "significant other" that I could pick up the phone and call or drop by his office to share the good news. I don't think I was necessarily crying for John, but for the fact that there wasn't a significant other in my life, whether it was John or someone else.

I would also dread the beginning of every school year. I would have to fill out all of the personal information sheets for each child. There was always a line for information on the child's father. Every year I would have to put "deceased." Each year I would think to myself, "Maybe next year I will have a name for that line?" It was the same thing for sports. I would try to get Brandon on a team where I knew some of the people so I didn't feel so awkward. At least if one person knew our story, I felt more comfortable.

The holidays seemed to get better with each year. I do know that the second Christmas was the hardest for me. Right before I was leaving for church on Christmas Eve, I received a phone call from one of my friends that had been with us in Cabo San Lucas when John died. This triggered flashbacks of John's death. I could not get past the images of his death. Every time I would shut my eyes, I would see his body bobbing in the ocean. Once I got to church, it was a struggle to not think about it. I regrouped until the priest started talking about Jesus being the "son without His Father." From then on, it was downhill and I cried through the whole service. I now realize that my first Christmas I "just got through it" and the second Christmas I actually experienced the holiday as a widowed single mom.

On occasion, I would still have my pity party. Fortunately, these episodes were short lived. On my third Christmas, I had one of these pity parties. It happened when I started receiving my annual Christmas cards. I really did enjoy getting cards from the people I only heard from at this time of the year, but at the same time it was also a reminder of what I no longer had. A reminder of my past life, and what I would have had. I would see all of my friends now out in private practice and expanding their families. I wanted so badly to have another child, and I knew if John had remained alive we would have had our third child, maybe even a fourth. I would think, "That should be me, but here I am still a single mom, not looking optimistic about adding to my family." Luckily for me, I had good dear friends that would bring me up during these down times and give me the reassurance that I needed.

One struggle that I still face is the fading of my memories. My life with John has become hazy. I have a hard time remembering our life together as a couple and as a family. I do not remember what it was like to have John as a husband and a father. It seems like a distant life that barely existed. I know no other life than the one that I have. John was never here to help with two children. My life with Brandon and Danielle is just that…my life, not our life. I never got to know what it would have been like to have John help me with both children.

In addition to "the firsts," another second year struggle was, "Who am I now?" "Where do I belong?" Once John died, I no longer felt as if I was part of the medical community. I did not feel as if I belonged anywhere! When I was married to John, I felt "normal." Now, most of my friends were married. I felt so lost. "Where do I go? What do I do?" I had so many unanswered questions. I was afraid of who I now was.

I was extremely lucky to have reunited with one of my best friends whom I had not talked to in probably four years. We had lost contact with each other, but John's death brought us back together. I had known her since junior high and we were college roommates. Needless to say, we share a lot of found memories. She was still single, which was my saving grace for my social life. She was the one person who would continue to invite me out when I didn't feel like it. Each time I would say, "No," I would thank her for asking me and tell her to keep asking because eventually I would say, "Yes." I did finally tell her "Yes", so she is the person responsible for reintroducing me to a social life that was not with other widowed people. A true friend does not give up on you and she didn't.

People will say that you are a different person since your spouse has died, but I can't say that. I am the same person, but John's death revealed qualities about me that I never knew I possessed. I am the same person as when John was alive, but now I have exposed parts of me that I was unaware existed. I have compassion, forgiveness, patience, faith, love, independence, and a deep appreciation for life. I feel I have so

much more to offer now as a person as a result of John's death.
Initially, when John died, I thought I had died too. I had to
adjust my way of thinking. Just because John had died didn't
mean I wasn't a whole person. John wasn't what made me
whole. I was what made me whole! I don't need a spouse in my
life to feel as if my life if complete. Only I can make sure I have
a fulfilling life. I am responsible for making my life enriched. It
is not contingent upon someone else.

At first, I didn't know where I belonged or who I was. I
didn't feel as if I fit in socially. I soon realized that I socially
"fit-in" however I chose. If I chose to be a recluse, then I would
be one. If on the other hand, I chose to get out and do something
with my life, that too would happen. It was all in my attitude! I
was an outgoing person when John was alive and by the grace
of God, this part of me didn't die along with him. Of course, this
part of me was "hidden" during those first several months. It
did take some time to reenter the social life. Part of this was
because I wasn't ready and I was consumed with my newborn
baby.

Once I was ready, then came dealing with dating and being
single again. Yikes! At the start of each WAY support group
meeting, I would usually open with a poem. One of the sessions
had to deal with hope and dating again. I didn't have anything
to read for this session, so I jotted down what I was feeling at the
time. I don't claim to be a poet, but this poem was the end result
of those thoughts.

There Is Hope

There is hope beyond this day.
There is hope I won't always feel this way.
There is hope that the pain will subside.

There is hope because I have the greatest Guide.
There is hope when the good days outnumber the bad.
There is hope that my children will have another dad.
There is hope when I can think that some day again I may be
a wife.
There is hope when I can say, "I love life!"

I have been able to look beyond my pain and suffering and find hope. Without hope, my life would have seemed meaningless. I had to cling to what little bit of hope I had those first few months. My hope was that one day my life would be normal again and I wouldn't always be so sad. This hope was what kept me going on those not so good days.

1 Timothy 5:14 So I counsel younger widows to marry, to have children, to manage their homes and to give the enemy no opportunity to slander. God spoke to me early on with this scripture. Even though marriage was not on my mind, He gave me hope through this scripture that one day I would remarry. I once believed remarriage was something that I would never consider, but I soon realized that I had a big heart with a lot of room for a lot of people. I was not wanting or expecting someone to fill John's shoes. That was unrealistic. I did want and expect to find someone to fill my heart with love and love my children as his own. I did not think this was unrealistic.

I think that since the initial pain of John's death had become foggy, was why I was considering marriage as part of my future. John's death can be compared to Danielle's labor. I know Danielle's birth hurt incredibly, but I would go through it again in order to have another baby. The same is with remarriage. I didn't want to be widowed again, but I would go through it again in order to love again. I wanted to be able to share my life with another man. No one would ever take John's place, but one day I knew I would love again. I also knew it would be a different love than the love I had with John, hopefully an even better love. Because I was an enriched person due to John's death, I had so much more to give a man.

Suddenly becoming single after John's death brought me face-to-face with changes I hadn't planned or desired. I thought the wedding ceremony guaranteed that I would "live happily every after," but there are no guarantees in life. When I left singleness for marriage, I never expected to return to it. This was a period of reorientation for me. It can be a positive time in a widowed person's life if he/she lets it.

I used this time in my life as a time to grow. I stepped out of my comfort zone and tried new things, such as putting together support group sessions, going out with single friends and even joining a gym. I also did quite a bit of reflective thinking and spiritual growth during this time. As a single again person, I had to change and get in touch with myself. Things were no longer the married life. I had to discover myself apart from marriage.

There is no formula or time frame for when to begin dating. I knew I needed to allow myself time to heal. If I hadn't waited until I was really ready, then I would have been in an unhealthy relationship. Group dates are a great way to start. I started out by going out with mixed company. I did quite a bit with both male and female friends from the support group. I, personally, felt I needed to wait one year before I started to date. There wasn't any particular reason for this time frame.

I probably should have waited longer, but I wanted to get that "first date" out of the way. It wasn't as bad as I thought. In fact, I really enjoyed myself and had fun. It was a double date, which was a good way to start out in the dating scene. Once I went out on one date, all of the sudden I had friends who had the "perfect person" for me to meet. I didn't let myself get into a serious relationship until two-and-a-half years after John's death. I do not think I was ready for one until this time. I had people who I had dated that would have liked to have a more serious relationship, but the timing wasn't right. Since being single again was a period of reorientation for me, it was important for me to not get serious with the first person that was interested in me.

I found that if I was confused about a relationship, then it wasn't God's will. If I felt this confusion, I would take some time away from the person and pray about it. When God sends the "right" person into your life, you feel a sense of peace and love. You don't wonder, "Is this Mr. Right?" If it is God's choice, He will bring the two of you together in His own timing. God had a purpose for my singleness. A serious relationship happened in His timing, not mine. When I was dating in "my time," I had problems. I would question myself. I would wonder, "Is this the right person for me? Am I ready for this?" Obviously, I wasn't ready for a relationship when I had all of these issues. However, when I waited on God's timetable it all seemed to fall in place for me.

I was open to remarriage, but it was not my goal in life. I wanted to find a friend before I found a partner. I had to gain the self-confidence to know that I could do it on my own…without a husband. I saw that I could take care of my children and myself. Something I never thought possible. I knew how precious the gift of love was. It is something to be cherished. I knew that when I remarried (that's when not if!), I would be a much better wife because I was more capable of expressing my love and appreciation for someone.

With John's death came the ability for me to love in a different way. It is a much deeper and genuine love than when I was younger. I looked forward to having that type of marriage one day. Remarriage is waiting on God to open the door and letting the right person into your life. God has his own timetable for all of us. I had to have the attitude "If I get married two years from now or ten years from now, it will be in God's timing." I had to trust in the Lord and let Him take care of it for me.

To love again is to risk losing again. Losing again was not something I wanted to ever experience again, but to not love again seemed even worse. I couldn't live in fear of what might happen. My life is in God's hands. I would let Him lead me. *John 8:12 I am the light of the world. Whoever follows me will never walk in darkness, but will have the light of life.* God has given me the light of life. When you love God, you radiate an inner beauty. God gave me the feeling of contentment with being alone. That didn't mean I was happy being alone, but I was "okay" with my situation. Again, I knew when the time was right that everything would fall into place in that area of my life.

I learned to live by *Psalm 37:7 Rest in the Lord and wait patiently on Him.* I had to wait on the Lord to let me know when I was ready for a relationship. He knew better than me when this should happen. Even though I didn't want to fear losing again, once God opened my heart to love again and let another man in it, those fears surfaced. I never thought I could love another man but John, but God opened my eyes to see it was possible. I know that I am not immune to tragedy and losing again could happen. I didn't want to be widowed again, but I also didn't want my life void of love. It is very special to have someone in my life to share my children's lives.

Earlier, I mentioned a boy at my son's baseball practice that complained to his father that Brandon "didn't know how to throw the ball." I cried to my boyfriend at the time that the little boy was right. He showed me such compassion. He came over that afternoon with his baseball glove and played ball with him in the backyard. I never asked him to do this. He did this on his own accord, which showed his sincerity. His dad died when he was eleven, so I think this made him much more compassionate toward Brandon. He does things with Brandon that he never did as a child. He even joined YMCA Indian Guides with him. Brandon is Braveheart and he is Strongheart. It is special for me to see Brandon have a relationship with another man.

I had to believe that God wouldn't take away except to give me back something better. I waited two-and-a-half years to have a serious relationship with another man, but it was well worth it. God placed a very special man in my life in His timing, not mine. *Romans 8:28 And we know that in all things God works for the good of those who love him.* I had to wait and see that God was going to make my painful situation into something good. I had to learn to embrace my pain because I knew that God would bless me with an even better love. I have to give God the glory for all of the blessings in my life.

Chapter Nine

New Beginnings, New Me

Isaiah 43:18 Forget the former things; do not dwell on the past.

With every ending in our life, we are brought to a new beginning. I had people pointing me in the right direction, but ultimately I was the one who had to take the journey. One Sunday, the minister at my church did a sermon about living in the present. He used the analogy of the rearview mirror in the car. The rearview mirror represented our past. He talked about how we had to occasionally look through the rearview mirror to see where we have been, but if we only drive using the rearview mirror we will crash. That is how my life has been. The rearview mirror has helped me to get to where I am going, but I had to look forward through the windshield of life to stay on track and not crash.

I chose not to be a victim of my circumstances. If I only looked through the rearview mirror and focused on my past, I would become a victim. I chose to focus on the present and not on my past. Focusing on the past would not have enabled me to be where I am right now in my life. Right now, I am able to reach out to others in similar situations. The Widowed and Young group is no longer active like when it first started, but I will continue to minister to others who are widowed and young if I receive their name and number. Writing this book is another avenue of outreach for me. I live in the present, but integrate my past to help people in the present.

In addition, I was also able to see that there was a lighter side to my loss. For instance, when I built my house, I built it for me, not John. I didn't do anything to my house because I thought it would be something John would have enjoyed. I chose everything that I would enjoy, since I was the one living in it. I can honestly say that John would not have gone along with the pastel floral print in my bedroom and bathroom, especially those pink and white towels! It was a great feeling to build the house for me. I wasn't trying to please anyone but me. It was a newfound freedom that I hadn't experienced in several years.

I will always remember and honor John by living my life to the fullest. Moving into my new house was a new life and new beginning for me. I finally felt some autonomy again. Once I made the move, it was as if my life had a new start. Of course, those first few months on our own, we still spent quite a bit of time at Grandma and Grandpa's having dinner. I hadn't cooked a family meal in so long that I was a bit apprehensive about my culinary skills. Once I got back into being a family again, my confidence was boosted. I started having friends over for dinner again. I figured I could test my cooking on them first!

Death has changed my whole perspective on life. My priorities are much different now. What used to be important to me before seems trivial now. Not having a perfect house isn't a priority anymore. I really don't care if the beds aren't made and there is some dirt on the floor. I don't try to be "super mom." With my son, Brandon, I made homemade baby food. With

Danielle, she ate the jarred baby food. I am not so focused on the material or superficial things in life. I am very thankful for everything that I have.

Being a single parent was not something that I planned or anticipated for in my life. What I thought would be an insurmountable task for me was something I did for five years. I loved my children during those five years of being a single mother just as much as any family that has both parents. Danielle used to tell people, "I have two daddy's in Heaven...God and my daddy, but God didn't die, daddy died in the ocean." Then she would go on how to say how God is in our hearts. Even though she was only four when she said this, she knew that she did not have a daddy that was physically present.

Happiness is something that you possess. You cannot go looking for it. Genuine happiness does not come from being single or married. It comes from within yourself when you begin to give yourself to others. I made the choice to be happy and not miserable. I had to acknowledge what had happened to me, accept that I could not change it and let it go. I am very thankful for being led to make that choice. Like I said earlier, I had people pointing me in the right direction, however, I ultimately had to take the journey to my road of happiness. *Proverbs 15:13 A happy heart makes the face cheerful, but heartache crushes the spirit.*

Chapter Ten

Spirituality/Faith

Psalm 107:1 Give thanks to the LORD, for he is good; His love endures forever.

Before John's death, I did not frequent church on a regular basis. I grew up in the Methodist church. I attended Sunday school and youth group, but then I was "too cool" to be in the youth group once the high school life hit me. In college, it was the same. I would much rather sleep late on Sunday morning than attend a church service.

Once I got married, we would go to church every once in a while, but not very often. We knew we would eventually move so we thought, "Why establish a temporary church, we will wait until we have a home base" or "that is John's only day off, I'm going to let him sleep late." There was always some excuse to not go to church. And if someone mentioned to me they couldn't meet me for lunch because they had Bible Study, I would roll my eyes at those "Holy Rollers." I had quite the attitude about these people, but guess what? Now I am one of "those people."

I will never forget the day I became one of "those people." My sister-in-law's husband, Bill came by to see me. This was about two weeks after John's death. Up until John's death, I had felt uncomfortable around Bill because I thought he was "too religious," but this time I was ready for him. I asked him, "What do I have to do to make sure I go to Heaven?" He told me, "You need to ask Jesus Christ into your heart." I asked him how to do this and he told me, "Just ask Him into your heart and believe that Christ died for your sins." That was when I truly accepted Christ into my life.

All of my life I had considered myself a Christian because I believed in God, prayed at night, and went to church on occasion. It took John's death for me to realize that I had not accepted God into my heart or life. It was hard to believe that God could forgive me for my past and my attitude toward dedicated Christians. Unfortunately for me, it took a tragedy to open my eyes to the Lord, but luckily they were opened. God surrounded me with many strong Christians right after John's death.

Since I wasn't involved with church or Bible Study before John's death, I didn't own a Bible. I was embarrassed to say that I didn't own one, but I was so hungry for the Word of God, that I didn't care. I asked my mom to take me to the Christian bookstore, so I could get one. When the clerk asked what "version" I would like, I had no idea. I said, "What do you mean?" She said, "There are different versions" and named a few. I had no idea, so I told her to give me what most people buy and that I wanted to be able to understand what I was reading. So, at the age of twenty-eight, I finally owned a Bible that I could read.

A strong faith lifted me above my tragedy and sorrow. I know what it is to have faith and believe in the healing power of prayer. I have learned the hard way that God does not promise to solve all of our problems, but he does promise to be with us always. His love is everlasting for those that believe. I had my life all planned for us. Unfortunately, the plan for my life was not God's plan. God's plans and our plans aren't always the same. I realized that my life was in God's hands and I couldn't live in fear of the "what-ifs" of life. I had to pray every night (and still do) that God help me to place all of my worries in His lap. My life became much easier once I could do this. All you have to do is trust in the Lord! I have found that when I release my worries to the Lord, he lightens my load!

I had so many questions about John's death that I was letting haunt me. I wanted to know why he didn't try harder to get out of the water. Three other men were able to make it out of the water alive. Why couldn't he? How could he give up? I have found that rather than torture myself with the "why's" I needed to pray for inner peace rather than the answers to all of these questions. *Numbers 6:26 The LORD turn his face toward you and give you peace.* The peace that I have felt has lifted me above my problems. I had to nurture this hope to keep this peace. Turning to God during my turmoil comforted me and gave me a feeling of peace within that is indescribable. I had to allow myself to put my life under the care and protection of our Almighty God. When I trusted in God, I felt at peace during my painful journey of recovery.

If you have a strong relationship with God, you will better be able to deal with your grief and move on with your life. I know that regardless of what cards are dealt to me in this life, that I will overcome them. The reason I know this is because: *Psalm 91:2 I will say to the LORD "He is my refuge and my fortress, my God in whom I trust."* In the midst of all of the grief that I may endure in this life, I know that God will be my fortress. God can and will give your life meaning and direction. All you have to do is ask. It is not always easy to ask, since we are so quick to want and try to "fix" things by ourselves. John's death and the grief that followed became my stepping-stones to my faith in Christ.

However, there are times when I take a step backward. Mother's Day seemed to be a hard time of the year for me those first few years. This surprised me. I would get all teary-eyed at church when I would see all of the women with their husbands who were able to celebrate that love with each other. I had to continually remind myself of the following scripture: *Philippians 3:13 Forgetting what is behind and moving toward what is ahead.* This was one of God's greatest gifts given to me during the healing process. I knew that I couldn't focus on the past. I had to focus on God or my life was much too complicated. Once I reminded myself that God was and is in control of my life, I could regroup. When I do this, I am filled with God's inner peace, love and contentment. When I would get wrapped up in "what should have been" I would totally lose my focus.

I feel that my strong faith enabled me to move through my grief more quickly than someone who does not turn to God. Pain can either make you mad at God or pull you closer to Him for relief. I turned to the Lord for comfort and found in Him the foundation for which I build my life. I have seen people widowed the same amount of time or longer that have not turned to God. They are not at the same place as I am. They are angry, bitter and fearful of the "what-ifs." I am thankful that God put such strong Christians in my life to enable this transformation for me.

A message from the scriptures can soothe my sorrows more than any anti-depressant. I found that on my really bad days, I could open the Bible and read the first thing that caught my eye. It would give me the comfort that I was seeking. God's love and

Word comforted my grieving heart. A strong faith in God will not erase one's sorrow, but if you let it, it will give you the strength to sustain you. Sustained by faith, I do the best that I can. I had my faith to support me during my crisis.

I have found that God can work good through life's bitterest experiences. Yes, John's death caused me a great deal of pain, but God has used John's death to bring me some of life's greatest joys, which is my appreciation for life. I am so thankful for my life and the life that I have with my children. I am very blessed to be alive and witness all of these wonders. I could have easily walked to the other side of the beach with John, but Divine Intervention save my life and Danielle's life too.

The loss and grief are with me forever, but as the grief changes, I go on with my life. The pain will eventually subside when you go on living. In order to go on living, I knew that I must trust in the Lord. If Job could trust God through all of his hardships, I knew I could too. *Job 14:7a At least there is hope for a tree; if it is cut down, it will sprout again.* I knew that God couldn't "fix" my pain, but he did give me the gift of a new life.

My time of grief has helped me to understand the depth of God's love. From it, I have a much deeper sense of compassion and understanding. I have learned to love and know God on a much deeper spiritual level. I know that I have God's love through both the good and bad times in my life. God never promised me a pain-free life that would be free of any sorrow. However, He does promise to comfort me. God wrapped His arms around me and comforted me during those difficult times. His love is an everlasting love.

Knowing God's love was the only reassurance I needed during my aloneness. I thank God for granting me the strength and courage to live through those difficult times. *Philippians 4:13 I can do all things through him who gives me strength.* I thank Him for carrying me during the most vulnerable times. I, especially thank Him for not giving up on me. It took me two years before I was consistently going to church. I had a hard time sitting through a church service without crying, so I wouldn't go.

John was raised Episcopalian. I had his funeral in the Episcopalian church. The service was so beautiful and uplifting. After the funeral I almost felt obligated to raise my children in the Episcopal Church, even though I knew nothing about the religion. I kept trying to go to one of Episcopal churches here in Arlington, but never felt comfortable. Finally, God enlightened me. I realized that it didn't matter whether I raised my children in the Episcopal Church or Methodist church as long as I was raising them "in the church." One day I decided to go back to the church I had attended as a child. As soon as I walked through those doors, I felt as if I was back home. It was a comfort for me to be there again. Again, this all happened in God's time. I don't think I would have been ready to walk through those church doors two years prior. God has the plans for my life and I have to allow for them to unfold in His time.

I know that there is something better beyond this day. The day before my daughter, Danielle's baptism, I got a glimpse of what may lie on the "other side." I was stressed about both John's family and my family being together due to the tension I had been experiencing with them. I fervently prayed that it all go smoothly. The night before the baptism, I closed my eyes and immediately saw a bright light. I kept trying to open my eyes because I knew that I wasn't asleep. Every time I tried to open my eyes, I would see the bright light again.

Once I could get past this bright light, I could see the bluest of blue skies with the greenest of grass and clean brick roads. It was so peaceful and tranquil for me to see this. When I would try to open my eyes, I would see the bright light again. This only lasted a few minutes. When it was over, I opened my eyes and sat up in bed. I knew that was a gift and sign from God that Danielle's baptism was going to be a good day.

I chose to have Danielle's baptism on what would have been my fifth wedding anniversary. I knew that I needed to keep this day in perspective. With John's death came the celebration of another life, Danielle's. My brother and his wife had a double christening for their daughter, Gianina, with Danielle. This was a very special and unforgettable day for all of us. Now, February 16th is no longer a wedding anniversary I mourn, but the day of my daughter's baptism that I celebrate.

Maybe eternity will disclose the purpose for John's death. John's death is only one piece of the puzzle in my life. Once I am at death's door, all of the pieces will be joined together. Right now I cannot spend or waste my time wondering how this piece fits into my life. It seems that each day the pieces fit more closely together for me. My life makes more sense now than it has in years. God has picked up these pieces of my life and formed a foundation of strength for me that in turn will bless others. What a gift!

Through God's eyes I had to remind myself the life that my other friends had was not the life God wanted for me right now. God had other plans for me. I know that because of John's death that I have touched more people's lives than I ever thought possible. God is using me as His vessel to reach out to others who are hurting. *1 Peter 4:19 So, when those who suffer according to God's will should commit themselves to their faithful creator and continue to do good..* God is working through me to give other widowed people hope.

My circumstances opened my heart to the Lord. Only through my love and trust in God have I been able to accomplish what I have in my life. I have to give God all of the glory. *1 Chronicles 16:2 Give thanks to the LORD, call on his name; make known among the nations what he has done.* God turned my loss into glory. I have been able to share how the Lord has worked in my life. What I viewed as a "mess" in my life has now turned into a ministry.

As my life goes on, I can see the many blessings that God has brought me through this tragedy. It is hard to fathom John's death a blessing, but it has brought me to places I would have never gone had John remained alive. It seems a cruel way to bring about blessings in my life, but again, God never promised me an easy life. Spiritually, I have grown in ways I never knew existed. We just need to remember to lean on our Best Friend, the Lord our Savior during times of crisis. *Isaiah 41:13 For I am the LORD your God, who takes hold of your right hand and says to you, do not fear, I will help you.*

AFTERWORD

On July 7, 2000, I married Pat Hennessy, the boyfriend mentioned in this book. Together we are raising Brandon and Danielle. Our wedding was a special one, where we all took vows to each other to make us one family. Danielle even sang Pat a song from *Psalty's All New Praise Party Two!* CD called *"Welcome to the Family."* It goes, *"Welcome to the family, we're glad that you have come to share your life with us. As we grow in love and may we always be to you what God would have us be a family always there to be strong and to lean on. May we learn to love each other more with each new day. May words of love be on our lips in everything we say. May the Spirit melt our hearts and teach us how to pray that we might be a true family."* Needless to say there was not a dry eye at the reception, including Pat's. It was very touching. God has blessed me with an even better love than I had imagined. My love for Pat is deep and genuine. He is a very loved and appreciated man. *Job 42:12 The Lord, Blessed the latter part of Job's life more than the first.* God is good!

Printed in the United States
1183800001B/122